A. M. Schlesselman

HANDYBOOKS FOR CHURCH SCHOOL LEADERS
Edited by Lewis J. Sherrill, Ph.D., D.D.
Professor of Religious Education,
Louisville Theological Seminary

IMPROVING YOUR SUNDAY SCHOOL

*Practical Suggestions for Superintendents, Pastors,
and Others Whose Duty It Is to Supervise
the Teaching of Religion in the
Local Church*

By
PAUL H. VIETH, B.D., Ph.D.

Superintendent of Educational Administration and Director
of Research of the International Council of
Religious Education
Author of "Teaching for Christian Living" and
"Objectives in Religious Education"

PHILADELPHIA
THE WESTMINSTER PRESS
1930

TO MY WIFE
VERNA MARIE VIETH

WHOSE CONSTANT COMPANIONSHIP IN SERV-
ICE HAS ENCOURAGED AND HELPED ME
TO KEEP CLOSE TO THE PROBLEMS AND
NEEDS OF THE AVERAGE SUNDAY SCHOOL

FOREWORD

WE have come to the end of a century and a
half of Sunday School history. During that
time the institution has undergone many changes.
Gradually the struggle for educational respectabil-
ity has gained ground. Gradually the Church has
come to a recognition of the strategic importance
of religious education. During the past quarter of
a century the work of the Sunday School has expanded to include not only Sunday-morning but also
Sunday-afternoon, Sunday-evening, and through-the-
week activities. This more comprehensive educational
program of the Church we call the Church School.

The Sunday School, however, continues to hold a
central place in the Church's expanding educational
program. This book has been written with a view
to helping those who have general responsibility for
conducting Sunday Schools to share creatively in this
process of building an educational program. The
work of the Sunday School superintendent has undergone significant changes in recent years. Much has
been written about his work as an executive. Very
little has been said about his work as a supervisor.
Yet there is no more important task to-day than
that of the *improvement of teaching*. It is the chief
purpose of these chapters to suggest to superintendents, pastors, departmental principals, and

others who are leaders of teachers, ways in which they may best carry on this supervisory work. These suggestions have grown out of practical experience in many local situations.

To name all those to whom the author is indebted for help in producing these chapters would require a long list. First of all, he would have to name the International Journal of Religious Education, for it conceived the idea of a series of articles on this subject, and granted permission to reproduce them here. Then he would have to name the half dozen Church Schools in which he has served as superintendent and director of religious education, which have furnished the laboratory for his experience. Last, he would have to mention the group of co-workers who have helped to shape the ideas and ideals which he holds for religious education. To all such, his sincere appreciation is extended.

PAUL H. VIETH.

February 5, 1930.

CONTENTS

9

Chapter I

THE WORK OF THE SUPERINTENDENT

John Duncan was frankly puzzled. For seven years he had been the superintendent of the Pleasant Valley Sunday School. His chief task had been that of leading the entire school each Sunday morning in the opening and closing exercises, and he had done it with a dignity and power which was the pride of the entire church. But in time the Beginners and the Primary children had been organized into separate departments, each with its own service of worship. He missed the little folks from the opening exercises, but the remaining group was sufficiently large to elicit all his talents. More recently, however, the Juniors, the Young People, and the Adults had all formed departments of their own, each with a separate department principal. What was there left for the superintendent to do? This was the question which puzzled John Duncan. It is a question which has puzzled many another superintendent in the face of the increasing tendency toward departmentalization.

Let no one shed tears of regret over the passing of the doubtful honor involved in leading the whole school in opening exercises. The place of the superintendent in the new program of the Church School is far more important. Instead of leading one service of worship, he is responsible for providing the leadership for a service in each department. He has become the head of an important educational enterprise. Instead of being the leader in a small part of the program, he is the leader of a whole group of leaders and teachers of pupils of all ages.

A MANY-SIDED TASK

Organization, administration, supervision—these are the three great words in the superintendent's vocabulary.

He must be an organizer, arranging pupils in working groups, enlisting teachers and assigning them to the places in which they may render their greatest service, and initiating programs so that effective education may take place. He must build the machine through which an adequate program of religious education may be given to the church. He must make the outreach of his school so effective that every possible person in the community will be drawn into its membership.

He must be an administrator. Programs and policies, like New Year's resolutions, must be carried out if they are to be effective. The superintendent is the man behind the scenes who makes the whole machine move without squeak or rumble. He, more than any other person in the school, must take charge of the whole program and make sure that it is going forward all along the line.

The Work of the Superintendent

He must be a supervisor. It is not enough to organize a school and put a program into operation. It must move forward with efficiency. There must be continual improvement. A weakness here, a failure there, must be remedied. The superintendent is responsible for attaining the highest product in Christian character, and toward this end he must bend all the resources of the school.

This little book is to deal primarily with the supervision aspect of the superintendent's work. It represents a field almost untouched by the majority of superintendents. Sunday Schools generally run at a much lower level of achievement than that of which they are capable. Thousands of them could be doubled in their efficiency if as much attention were given to their *improvement* as is now given to maintenance of what already exists. Too many workers are self-satisfied. The work of supervision can lift the whole tone of teaching to a higher level.

It is difficult to separate supervision from the other phases of the superintendent's work. When he studies the work of a department, discovers needs, and proceeds to meet those needs, he has engaged in supervision, organization, and administration. We shall not quibble about terms in these pages. We want to be just as helpful as possible to superintendents. Often we shall need to venture into organization and administration in order to build a background for our discussion on supervision; but we shall always bear in mind that our primary purpose is to give help in this newer phase of work, that of improving the Sunday School.

At this point a word is in order as to the terms we shall use. Gradually a tendency has been growing to use Church School to mean the entire educational work of the church, such as Sunday School, Vacation School, Young People's Societies, clubs, pastor's classes, and so forth. The Sunday work of this Church School is coming to be spoken of as the Sunday Church School, to distinguish it from the Week Day Church School and the Vacation Church School. We shall deal here primarily with the Sunday Church School, because, in the vast majority of churches, this institution still holds the center of the educational stage. We shall use the old-fashioned name *Sunday School* because it is so familiar to everyone. Wherever necessary we shall point out the relation of the superintendent's work to the Church School in the wider sense.

WHAT IS SUPERVISION?

Factories and commercial concerns recognize that at best they will run below one hundred per cent efficiency. A corps of workers is employed to supervise what others are doing. These foremen, superintendents, or whatever their titles may be, do not assist in actually doing the work of the organization. They are employed to help to make the work of others

14

more efficient. Their work has been well done when there is a maximum output at a minimum cost. If it is true that a factory needs supervision in order to run at highest efficiency, how much more true it is of an educational institution.

What, then, is supervision? It is best defined by describing its purpose. The most helpful phrase we have found to describe the purpose of supervision is "improvement of teaching." Suppose that the general executive management of the Sunday School has done all it can to make teaching possible: the teachers and leaders have been placed in charge of groups of pupils to accomplish the work of education. Is anything more needed? Yes! There must be constant attention to the improvement of the work which is being done. This is supervision.

By supervision in the Sunday School, then, we mean that activity which has for its purpose the improvement of the work of all the teachers and officers to the end that greater results in pupil character may be brought about. If, by the efforts of one or a few persons set aside for supervision, the efficiency of the entire school may be lifted to a higher level, then we have abundant justification for promoting a program of supervision. Such results may be brought about by improving the teachers themselves, improving the working conditions, or improving the attitude of the pupils. Once we get in mind the simple idea that it is our business to improve the work

15

of teaching, countless ways of achieving this will suggest themselves.

Let us look at a few cases of what has been done by way of supervision in certain Sunday Schools:

A superintendent asked the principals of all departments of his Sunday School to accompany him on an observation tour to a neighboring Sunday School which was reputed to be very fine. On that Sunday the substitute principals presided in the home school. Each principal visited a department corresponding to his own. Following the visit, a report was made in a meeting of the workers' conference. Some things observed were commented upon favorably, and some things unfavorably. The workers received new ideas while at the same time they deepened their respect for their own school. The visit was more instructive than a course of training might have been. This superintendent was supervising.

A very vital problem in improving the work of teachers is the development of the proper attitude toward the work they are doing. Commendation of work well done is a stimulus to better effort. We all desire the feeling of satisfaction in the task we are doing. One superintendent follows the plan of writing each teacher a letter on his birthday. In this letter he does not simply express the usual congratulatory generalities but makes specific mention of the faithful work which the teacher has done and commends him for it.

From time to time, Sunday Schools adopt new lesson materials. Most of the newer materials are built on an educational theory different from that of the older type of lessons. Hence, unless careful preparation has been made, confusion is apt to result when the teachers first attempt to use them. It was in such a situation, after the teachers had had an opportunity to realize the problems involved in using the new material, that a superintendent asked his Junior principal to call together the teachers of that department. The subject for the conference was the new lesson materials. In answer to the numerous questions raised by the teachers, it was possible for him to give them some idea of the new curriculum approach. Time was taken to analyze the new materials rather carefully and to give each worker the key to understanding the materials which it was his business to use. Needless to say, this conference was a long step toward improving the teaching in this Junior Department.

In spite of all we may do, it is often the teachers who need training most who will not attend training schools or institutes. One superintendent approached this problem on the theory that if the workers will not go to places where training is to be had, it may be possible to take training to them. His monthly workers' conference was well attended by all teachers. He converted this conference into an educational venture in which the International Standard for the

Church School formed the basis of discussion. Through a series of meetings the various requirements of this Standard were discussed and applied to their particular school. In connection with the use of the Standard various outside readings were assigned and used for discussion in the group. This resulted in improved work in that school.

A board of religious education in a certain local church came to the conclusion that many difficulties would be overcome if parents would take a more encouraging attitude toward the Sunday School. After much discussion it was decided that the school had perhaps not given the parents an adequate opportunity to become acquainted with the work that was being done. Plans were made for a parent-teacher supper. The purpose of this supper was twofold: first, that parents and teachers might become better acquainted; and, second, that there might be brought before the group some of the ideals for which the Church School stands. The supper was an outstanding success. Many parents expressed their appreciation of the opportunity given them to learn more about the work in which the Sunday School was engaged. Following the supper, there were evidences that parents had assumed a larger responsibility for coöperation in the religious education of their children. In promoting this event the chairman of the Committee on Religious Education was practicing good supervision.

The Work of the Superintendent

In another church a director of religious education made a somewhat different approach to secure the coöperation of parents. He had the school adopt the use of report cards to be sent quarterly to the parents of each pupil. In addition to marks on the various phases of work that were being pursued in the school, the cards also carried records of attendance and tardiness. The plan succeeded in producing an appreciable effect on the attitudes of parents. Moreover, it had a wholesome effect on the attitudes of the teachers, for they soon discovered that if they were to mark grades at the end of the quarter they must keep in close touch with the work which the pupils were doing. This was entirely a by-product of the original plan.

A very young teacher was the best person who could be secured for Primary principal in a certain school. Her worship programs were far from satisfactory. It was the problem of the superintendent to secure an improvement in these programs. His approach involved visiting the department and making suggestions to the principal, putting helps for building worship programs into her hands from time to time, and, on one occasion, at the suggestion of the principal, conducting the program by way of demonstration.

The board of religious education in a given church came to the conclusion that its Sunday School work was far enough advanced to justify a new emphasis upon a more vital curriculum. The leading workers from the various departments were invited to join a committee for purposes of discussion of this important question. A period of one year was allowed for preparation before any considerable changes were made. The director of religious education, who served as the leader of this board, took occasion to attend a summer school in order to form a closer acquaintance with the problems of curriculum and available materials. When the changes in curriculum were made, the success of the venture was already assured because in each department there was a nucleus of workers who knew the meaning of the changes and were able to do the thing which was expected of them.

IS SUPERVISION PRACTICAL?

These examples of supervision in the Sunday School could be multiplied indefinitely. A sufficient number has been given to indicate that in every Sunday School there are some things of a supervisory nature which can and must be done. If supervision is not practical in the Sunday School, then we are indeed in a hopeless state of affairs. There is not a single school which does not need a large measure of improvement in the work which it is doing. The time has come when superintendents and other leaders must acquire the viewpoint that it is their duty not simply to set an organization going but to give continuous supervision in order that improvements may be made. Sometimes one approach will be successful, sometimes another. No superintendent will be able to use all the supervisory devices; let him do that which he can best do to improve the work of his school.

There are many ways in which a school may be improved. The superintendent who has a high ideal of the way in which work ought to be done will constantly see opportunities for improvement. One of the basic methods, which must be constantly emphasized, is the better training of teachers. A weakness which has developed in the school may be remedied through discussion in the workers' conference. Class visitation and conferences with teachers are always helpful, provided the superintendent feels competent to undertake this type of work. Sometimes the quality of Sunday School work may be revolutionized by adopting a better system of records or securing a more efficient secretary. Or it may be that reorganization of classes or departments, or even such a simple matter as the rearrangement of a room, will provide better working conditions and lead to a greater spiritual result. Visits to other schools to observe good work, proper equipment, and adequate building facilities, may be the means of bringing about improvement in the local school.

WHO SHALL SUPERVISE?

In these discussions we shall consider our problem largely from the standpoint of the superintendent. We have in mind the average school where the superintendent is the chief executive officer. In schools where there is an employed director of religious education, much more thorough work in supervision can, of course, be accomplished. In every church the pastor should be depended upon for help in the task of improving the school. While the pastor's attention to the work on Sunday may be limited because of other duties, he has so vital a contact with the whole task of the church that there are many things of a supervisory nature in which he can help throughout the week. In some communities it is possible to enlist the help of persons trained and experienced in public-school work. If such persons are teaching in the Sunday School it may be most profitable to release them for a more important task of supervising a group of workers.

The test of the superintendent's work is that of growth in Christian living. This is the great product of the school toward which all must labor. A secondary test of the work of the superintendent is the kind of workers he has enlisted and the spirit in which they perform their work.

CHAPTER II

THE BOARD OF RELIGIOUS EDUCATION

One of the first and most important steps in improving the Sunday School is to make it a legitimate child of the church. We mean by this that the church should recognize the Sunday School as a part of its own program of work and take the responsibility for it. Too often it has been detached and independent, while the main program of the church passed by on the other side. It must be not simply *in* the church, but also *of* the church and *by* the church. There is increasing emphasis on a church-centered program of religious education. The first step toward making religious education an integral part of the work of the church is to make its leadership *responsible to the church*.

A BOARD OF RELIGIOUS EDUCATION

The usual practice in many churches is to elect a superintendent for the Sunday School and then cease to worry or think about this office until the superintendent resigns or dies of old age or exhaustion. He is the head of the Sunday School with full power. If he is a strong-willed man, he will rule with an iron hand and make himself the lord of all he surveys. If he is more mild in manner, his kingdom will be a benevolent autocracy, with freedom granted here and there to share in the enterprise. If he is lacking in organizational sense and executive ability, each department and class will be free to do what is right in its own eyes and a disorganized confusion will result. He is not required to report to the church. He holds a term of office suited to his own pleasure. True, he may be reëlected from year to year, but woe be to the church which decides to change its leadership at such an annual election without the sincere request of the leader! Whole families and tribes have been known to withdraw from a church because it saw fit to end the term of office of the head of the family. We refrain from describing the conditions in the churches where the responsibility for religious education is so far removed from official sanction that the election of the head of the Sunday School is dependent upon a self-constituted body of Sunday School teachers, or—spare us the agony of the thought—upon the pupils.

A church board of religious education is the solution for this problem. It will make Christian education a definite part of the church's work. It will provide a more competent leadership than is possible through a single individual. It will make possible a development and expansion of the work now done by the Sunday School far beyond the ability of the Sunday School officers working alone. No church is too small or too backward to have such a board of religious education and to profit by it.

The Board of Religious Education

This chapter is devoted to a discussion of the board of religious education, its purpose, make-up, and work. We introduce the discussion here because we believe that any program for Sunday School improvement must rest on a sound foundation, and a working board of religious education furnishes such a foundation. Few churches have yet adopted this form of organization. It should become the purpose of every pastor and superintendent to establish such a board and set it to work. After the board is elected, both pastor and superintendent should take a large responsibility for guiding it into fruitful fields and for carrying out the program which it authorizes.

VALUE OF A BOARD

Some of the advantages of a church board of religious education may be enumerated as follows:

1. It makes religious education officially a part of the total program of the church and dignifies it by putting it under responsible leadership.

2. It convinces the church of the importance of religious education by making provision for it in a dignified way.

3. It provides for democracy with authority, by electing members to a board, and then vesting ample power in that board.

4. It makes possible the placing of religious education under a representative body through careful selection of the members of the board.

5. It gives the officers of the school the support of a responsible body, which will authorize their work and hear reports upon it. A new venture is more likely to succeed when it has been first accepted and adopted by a board.

6. It makes executive action easier because it is less personal. It is easier for a board to discharge an incompetent worker than for an individual to take such drastic action; this is true also of advocating programs of improvement which may at first be unpopular.

7. It enhances the importance of the work in the minds of the officers and teachers, through the official appointment of workers by the board.

8. It provides a group which is lifted above the routine of school administration and therefore is in a position to give attention to policies and programs in a broad sense.

9. It provides for continuity in policies without the risk of a complete upsetting of the ongoing program when there is a change in pastor, superintendent, or other executive leader.

10. It provides an agency through which the church may express itself in community movements for religious education.

HOW SHALL THE BOARD BE CONSTITUTED?

How shall a board of religious education be constituted? It should be small enough to make effective work possible. A board of five to seven regular members is suggested. Authority may be given to the board to call in a few associate members because of special contributions which they may be able to make. For example, one board added to its membership the principals of departments—that is, those not already elected as regular members—so as to establish a close contact with the work in each department.

Who should be on the board of religious education? The obvious answer to this question is: those best qualified to serve in this capacity. The five or seven best-qualified persons in any church will constitute a competent board for that church. They need not necessarily be working in the Sunday School, though familiarity with the problem at hand has its advantages. There may, however, be competent persons in the church who for good reasons are not available for service on Sundays but might nevertheless render valuable service on such a board—for example, a mother with public-school and religious-education experience. The pastor, the director of religious education, and the Sunday School superintendent should be members ex officio of the board. All other members should be elected to the board because of their special fitness, not because of the job they happen to hold in the church or Sunday School, except as provision may be made for associate members. If this rule is not observed, there is danger that the board will be lost in the petty details of organization and administration without giving adequate attention to the larger policies of the church. Unless there is a competent layman available for the office, the pastor should serve as chairman of the board.

Some denominations specify the manner in which the body responsible for religious education in the local church shall be chosen. In most cases, however, the individual church will have to decide upon its own method. One way is to have the board of religious education elected by the congregation. This brings religious education forcibly before the church, and dignifies it as one of the major tasks of the church. Another plan is to have the board appointed by the governing body of the church. Since this official body may be thought of as representing the entire church program, this plan tends to emphasize and unify that program. Some churches have wisely provided that the chairman of the board of religious education shall be a member ex officio of the official board of the church, still further assuring unity in the church's program. Whatever plan is adopted it is important that the board should regularly bring its work to the attention of the governing body of the church.

It is a good plan to elect the members for a set period of years—three, for instance—and so to arrange the terms of office that a minority of them expire each year. For example, to get started with a board of seven members, two might be elected for one year, three for two years, two for three years, and thereafter each new member elected for a period of three years. This will provide for continuity.

WHAT THE BOARD SHOULD DO

Having suggested how the board of religious education should be constituted, let us inquire into its work in greater detail. Let us remember that this is a body with authority, designated by the church to be responsible for its *entire* educational program. This means more than maintaining what already exists. It means a constant effort directed toward the very best and most comprehensive program of religious education which the church is capable of maintaining. "It must do more than operate the present school on traditional lines; it must create the public opinion and win the support which will make possible a new school operated in harmony with the most approved modern methods. It must convict the church of pedagogical sin against her children and then show it what to do to be saved." [1]

1. STUDY ITS WORK. The board of religious education must make a constant study of the best theory and practice in religious education as well as of the present program of its church. A study of the best theory, in the light of present practice, will reveal the points where improvements should be made. Such improvements cannot all be made at

---

[1] Athearn, W. S., "The Organization and Administration of the Church School," page 270. The Pilgrim Press, Boston, 1917.

once. Some may require several years of study, preparation, and planning. When once they have been brought to the board for consideration, however, there is hope that ultimately aspiration will be crowned with success. For example, the discovery of a lack of efficient workers may lead to a program of training; the recognition of the inadequacy of time available at present may lead to the organization of a Vacation Church School; the recognition of an inadequate number of rooms may lead to plans for remodeling or for erecting a new building.

2. EDUCATE THE CHURCH. A second duty of the board of religious education is that of educating the entire church constituency to the need of religious education. It will avail little to have a small group get the ideal of new and better things, unless this vision can be passed on to the entire church. Through reports, special programs, sermons, articles in the church paper, presentation before groups of the church, and so forth, this educative process should be kept constantly alive and active.

3. ORGANIZE THE SCHOOL. The board must provide the church with an effective organization for religious education. This means, first, the organization of the larger phases through which a modern program of religious education comes into being— Sunday Church School, Vacation Church School, pastor's classes, and so forth; and the proper integration of the programs of these various agencies. It

means, second, effective organization within each of these phases of the program, such as the Sunday Church School. Much of the work of the latter will of course be performed by officers appointed for this purpose, but it must be carried out under the direction of the board.

4. PROVIDE LEADERSHIP. The board should exercise the final authority in selecting the leaders for the entire Church School. If there is to be an employed director of religious education, he should be elected by the board, and all other workers elected on his nomination. Where there is no employed director, as is the case in the majority of churches, the chief officers, such as the superintendent of the Sunday Church School and the principal of the Vacation Church School, should be elected by the board, and all other workers should be elected by the board on nomination of these chief officers. Every officer and teacher should be elected for a period of one year, so that once every year the working staff may be thoroughly considered.

5. BUILD A PROGRAM. A very important task of the board of religious education is that of building an adequate program to meet the religious needs of the pupils of the school. The planning of various activities and the selection of courses of study must receive careful attention. While many parts of the program will originate with the workers, no significant activities or changes in courses of study should

be undertaken without the authorization of the board. Only thus will it be possible to achieve proper balance and integration for the program of the entire school.

6. SUPERVISE THE WORKERS. After electing a working staff, the board must give consideration to the task of providing the kind of supervision which will assure the most effective work. This involves both the improvement of the workers and the improvement of working conditions. Workers' conferences, training classes, provision for libraries, and any kind of assistance to teachers in their tasks would come under this general heading.

7. PROVIDE GOOD WORKING CONDITIONS. The board should assume as another of its tasks that of providing proper educational equipment to meet the needs of the school. Most Church Schools are woefully lacking in this respect. It is only through constant study and planning that the need will be adequately met. Demands for equipment which may come from individual workers should be judged in the light of the total needs of the school.

8. COÖPERATE WITH OTHER CHURCHES. The board should inquire into the possibilities for strengthening its work through coöperative relations with the other churches of the community, in leadership training, week-day religious education, and so forth. In all such relationships the board should represent the church.

9. HEAR REPORTS. Finally, the board will be con-

cerned about hearing reports of progress from those
to whom it has assigned responsibility. The superintendent of the Sunday School and others in responsible positions should be expected regularly to bring
reports on the work being done. The board should
give ample time for the evaluation of such reports,
consideration of recommendations made, and, on the
basis of such reports, guidance in future programs.

THE BOARD AT WORK

The best machine in the world is of no value unless
it works. This is true also of a board of religious
education in the church. Merely setting up such a
board will not solve our problems. The board must
actually undertake its task and work at it seriously
and continuously.

In the first place, the board must organize by electing a chairman and a secretary. Minutes should be
kept of each meeting so that the work may be progressive and continuous. The chairman should be the
best man available, one who can lead a discussion
without dominating it, get meetings started and
stopped on time, and rally his coworkers in the common undertaking. Meetings of the board should be
held at least once a month on a stated date. Enough
time should be allowed for each meeting to permit
unhurried attention to the work.

It should be recognized that a board does not run
itself. Whenever an outstanding piece of work is

done by a board, one may rest assured that back of it stands an individual who has done some preliminary thinking and outlined the problems so that the board may have a task on which to spend its labor—furnished the grist, so to speak, for the mills of the board. No board of religious education will accomplish a great deal if it simply meets, trusting that problems and their solution will be thought of as the session progresses. Some one person must, between sessions, carry on his mind and heart the work of the board.

If the church has an employed director of religious education he should stand in the relationship of executive officer to the board. He should bring to it the problems for consideration, and carry out its decisions. The board in this case will become largely an authorizing, evaluating, and reviewing group, with tasks of the highest importance. In cases where there is no employed director of religious education, the board will need to assume larger responsibility for initiating policies and programs. But there must still be some one who will take the lead in guiding the activities of the board. If the pastor is active in the work of the Sunday School, he is the logical person to assume this responsibility. In fact, many pastors are so fully realizing their responsibilities toward religious education that they are virtually serving as directors of religious education. This is a hopeful tendency. The superintendent of the Sunday School should also be expected to furnish "grist" for the "mill" of the board, at least so far as it touches the Sunday School, which in most churches is the major part of the board's task. The chairman of the board may also be looked to for guidance in developing the work of the board. At any rate, he must take responsibility for integrating into a comprehensive program of work the various items which clamor for the attention of the board.

The board of religious education will find plenty of things of great importance which must be done when once these ideas are accepted: (1) it is responsible to the church for developing a comprehensive program of religious education, and (2) it must pass upon every important matter relating to the development of that program before it may be carried into effect. Many churches bear testimony to the great value they have received from putting their programs of religious education into the hands of such a board.

THE BOARD AND THE WORKERS' CONFERENCE

There may be those who are asking, What should be the relation of the board of religious education to the monthly workers' conference? The workers' conference will be dealt with in Chapter V. Suffice it to say here that its primary purpose is the education of the workers and not the consideration of matters of business or administration. It will be a good policy, however, for the board to bring to the workers' conference for discussion such new policies as will affect the whole school. Such, for example, would be the adoption of a new system of records. The purpose of such discussions is merely educational, and the

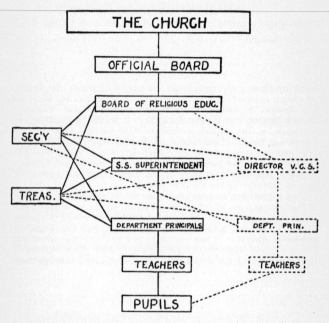

This diagram shows a possible form of organization for the Church School under a board of religious education. The official board may or may not be placed between the congregation and the board of religious education. The heavy lines indicate the form of organization for the Sunday School. The dotted lines show what the plan might be if the church also has a Vacation Church School. Other agencies might similarly be shown in the chart. Note that the superintendent of the Sunday School and the principal of the Vacation Church School are each directly responsible to the board, and that the

group of workers will not decide whether or not such
records should be adopted, but the board will at all
times have a sympathetic ear turned to the wishes and
ideas of the group of workers as a whole. The workers in their several departments should also be encouraged to initiate recommendations and bring them
to the board.

---

work of these two agencies is correlated through the board.
If closer correlation can be effected through having some of
the Sunday School workers teaching also in the Vacation
Church School, this is very desirable. It would be particularly
fortunate if the superintendent of the Sunday School were
competent to act also as head of the Vacation Church School
and were so situated that he would have time to do so. The
relationship of the secretary and the treasurer to both phases
of work indicates that there is one budget and one system of
records for the entire Church School.

This church has no employed director of religious education.
If there were such an officer, his position would be immediately
below the board of religious education. He would probably
serve the Sunday School as superintendent and the Vacation
School as director. Lines would be drawn from the secretary,
treasurer, and department principals to him, thus indicating
that the work of the entire school is coördinated through him.

Chapter III

IMPROVING THE TEACHERS

The best way to improve teaching is to improve the teachers. Superintendents have rightly made their greatest concern the securing and holding of a group of able and consecrated teachers. What they have not always so clearly seen is that to have a group of good teachers requires more than the selection of the best available workers. It involves their training as well. Constant vigilance and unceasing effort is the price which must be paid if you would have a staff of competent teachers.

The superintendent's responsibility for the improvement of teachers may be considered under four headings: Enlistment of Workers, Installation of Workers, Sharing the Workers' Problems, Training Workers in Service. In the departmentalized school this work of the superintendent should always be carried out in close coöperation with the department principals. They should be regarded as the superintendent's administrative and supervisory staff. The pastor should also be regarded as an important member of the official family of the school, and he will often be able to do the things which no lay worker could accomplish.

ENLISTMENT OF WORKERS

The number of persons required to run a modern Sunday School puts a severe strain on the church membership for competent workers. In the main, it may be said with confidence that the group of Sunday School workers represents the finest people in any church. Yet in most churches there are many persons who have not been enlisted in the teaching work who would make splendid workers if some one would discover them and interest them in the idea. The superintendent and his staff must constantly be on the lookout for such workers. Here is an illustration of careful work on the part of a superintendent.

It had all happened so quickly! Ella Blackburn could scarcely realize that she was now a Sunday School teacher. To-morrow morning she would have to be ready to teach a class of seven-year-olds! She was more than a little pleased with the idea, but she was also afraid.

It had all come about in this way. There had been a Young People's banquet at the church, to which she had gone. By merest accident, so it seemed, she had been placed at the table next to John Garfield, the Sunday School superintendent. She had never met him before, but he had been so friendly that they were soon well acquainted. He had seemed so interested in her—wanted to know what she did, where she had gone to school, what books and magazines she read, and what she thought on this or that religious question. At the time she had attached no particular significance to these questions. She had been more than a little flattered. She had said to her mother that night, "He is a man who takes a girl seriously, and assumes that she uses her head for something more than carrying a hat!"

Two weeks later the principal of the Primary Department had called at Ella's house. Almost before she was seated she had said, "Miss Blackburn, you know that Mrs. Johnston you sometimes see at church? She has been teaching in our Primary Department. She has a class of the dearest youngsters, and they all like her. But her husband has not been well, and she has had to give up her class. I came to invite you to take it!"

Ella had been so surprised that she could hardly stammer her answer. She had quickly protested that she could not do it because she had had no experience. Yet when the principal had persisted, she had ended by agreeing to give the matter a try. And she had meant to put her very best into that try!

Thus had Mr. Garfield taken the first steps toward developing a new teacher for his Sunday School. He realized that Miss Blackburn lacked training and experience. But he knew also that the chances of making her into a good teacher would be much better if he should get her started in some activity and help her to prepare herself as she went along than if he should require her to take a course of training before letting her serve. Training is, of course, essential. Whenever possible it should be sought as one of the qualifications for teaching. But there are times when training may best be given "on the job."

It is among the older pupils that the superintendent should seek most hopefully for prospective teachers. The school, if it has done its work well, has already developed the right attitude among these young people. It has given them a chance to show their spirit in acts of service within their classes and departments. Courses in training may be made a part of their regular work. Those who, by ability, interest, and previous record, give promise of making good workers, should be given special training for leadership during their later high-school years. Such preservice training will not do more, however, than get them started in their work. The problems they will meet when they assume positions of leadership will require constant training while they are in service. If a Sunday School would make it a policy consistently to prepare its pupils for service in the school and church, there would be a tremendous difference in the quality of leadership in the course of a few years.

INSTALLATION OF WORKERS

With many superintendents the work of enlisting teachers is considered completed when the person in question has agreed to take a class. Often the request is made in such a way as to minimize the importance of the task. If the objection is raised by the prospective worker that he is too busy, the superintendent is likely to answer, "But it will not take much time." If he objects that he is not prepared, the superintendent is likely to answer, "But the children are so young that it is not difficult." Consequently the new teacher is likely to begin his work thinking that it is not of very great importance.

One of the most effective ways of leading workers to sense the importance of the responsibility which they have undertaken is a public service of installation.[1] When Miss Blackburn, after hearing an effective sermon on the importance of the teaching ministry of the church, stood before the congregation and promised to give faithful service to the children of the church in the name of her congregation, something happened to her which made the task look very different from the way it had looked when she first promised to take a class. When she heard the congregation with one voice acclaim the importance of the task which these workers had undertaken, and promise as parents and church members to do their utmost to uphold the hands of those who were engaged in the sacred task of teaching, she felt sweeping through her soul a new feeling of kinship with the entire congregation and with the eternal purposes of God.

From experience the writer has learned that it is easier to enlist workers by laying before them the

---

[1] See Appendix A for a suggested service of installation and consecration.

tremendous challenge of the thing which they are to do than by minimizing the importance of it. Through pointing out to the prospective worker that it is a privilege which is offered him, and that in his turn he must give loyal service if he is to remain a member in good standing, he is led into his work with the right attitude. A frank talk between the superintendent and every new worker should invariably be a part of each new appointment.

Various methods have been used successfully to enhance the importance of the teacher's work, and dignify the appointment. One of these is the teacher's contract, whereby the teacher, in return for the privilege of teaching in the Sunday School, agrees to do certain things on his part. Obviously such a contract must first be made a voluntary matter to avoid any taking of offense. It may however be introduced gradually by appealing to the workers to make the conditions of the contract their purpose, and to signify this by signing on the dotted line. An illustration of such a contract is given herewith.

Agreement

In consideration of my election by the Board of Religious Education of Saint Peter's Church School and of the opportunity offered me to participate in the sacred work of teaching the religion of our Lord and Master, as a teacher or as an officer, I agree on my part that:

1. I will accept and faithfully perform the duties of that office, from this date to the following September 15.

2. I will make it a practice to attend the sessions regularly,

and if, for a real reason, I am prevented from coming, I will notify my department principal (or the superintendent) and help to provide a substitute who is mutually acceptable. If I am absent more than 10 Sundays in the year, or 3 Sundays without notice, I understand that my office shall be considered vacant.

3. I will make it a practice to come on time to the sessions, which I interpret to mean that as a teacher or officer I am to be present at least 10 minutes before the opening of the session.

4. I will prepare thoroughly for each session, maintain discipline, help to create an attitude of reverence and a spirit of loyalty and coöperation, and, with the help of God, set a good example in Christian living.

5. I will coöperate with the officers of the school, my department principal, and my fellow teachers; I will welcome constructive criticism and helpful suggestions, and will at all times abide by such rulings as may be made for the best interests of the whole school.

6. I will regularly attend the meetings of teachers and officers, known as the educational conference, and participate in the work of the conference.

7. I will broaden my knowledge of and experience in my task through reading and study. I will read regularly a magazine dealing with my work, study good books, or take a training course—all three if possible.

8. I will make a careful study of the "Self-Rating Score Card" adopted for our school, and make a conscious effort to measure up as high as possible on each of the points.

9. In case I find it impossible to continue my services for any reason, I will notify the department principal or the superintendent in writing at least two weeks in advance.

Signed: ....

Elmhurst, Illinois.

Another method is that of a teacher standard, or self-rating scale. If this is worked out coöperatively by the workers it will have great value. The illustration given herewith was worked out by the workers' conference of the author's Sunday School and revised by a class in the supervision of religious education. Any local church which desires to make use of this standard will do well to give the workers a chance to discuss it fully and revise it to the point where all can agree to it.

YOUR SELF-RATING SCALE

	Possible Score	Your Score
1. WORSHIP:		
a. Do you attend at least one worship and preaching service a Sunday, unless hindered by some real reason?	5	....
b. Do you make the worship service of your department in the Sunday Church School one of real worship for yourself, and so conduct yourself that you would be willing to have all the pupils follow your example?	5	....
c. Do you practice personal fellowship with God, with at least some moments each day dedicated specifically to this purpose?	5	....
2. LESSON PREPARATION:		
a. Do you devote a minimum of at least one hour a week to lesson preparation, getting thorough understanding of the content for yourself, and for your individual pupils?	12	....
b. Do you make a written teaching plan to use in the presentation of your lesson?	8	....
3. COÖPERATION:		
a. Do you relate your work to the whole church program, and are you interested in the other church activities of your pupils?	5	....
b. Are you open-minded in giving and receiving suggestions in conference with your officers?	5	....

	Possible Score	Your Score
4. PERSONAL RELATIONSHIPS TO PUPILS:		
a. Do you keep personal information about your pupils, such as addresses, telephone numbers, birthdays, and so forth, and such information about their work as will give you at all times an accurate picture of each individual?	5	....
b. Are you a real friend to your pupils, greeting them on the street, playing with them when opportunity offers, visiting them when sick, and taking an interest in their affairs?	5	....
c. Do you visit the homes of your pupils at least once a year, and is each absence checked by yourself or some responsible person?	5	....
5. FAITHFUL ATTENDANCE:		
a. Do you regularly attend the monthly workers' meeting and all departmental meetings?	10	....
b. Are you always present at 9.20 each Sunday morning in order to meet the first comers to your class?	10	....
c. Do you always give ample notice of necessary absence?	10	....
6. GROWTH IN EFFICIENCY:		
a. Do you read regularly at least one good magazine on your Church School work?	2	....
b. Do you make use of your Church School library, reading at least one good book annually on your work?	2	....
c. Do you complete one or more courses in a leadership-training class or school each year?	6	....
(We suggest also that visiting the corresponding grade in the public school is very helpful for growth in efficiency.)		
Total possible score	100	....

A teacher scoring between 90 and 100 may be known as a grade "A" teacher.

A teacher scoring between 80 and 90 may be known as a grade "B" teacher.

A teacher scoring between 70 and 80 may be known as a grade "C" teacher.

A teacher scoring under 70 is known as a grade "D" teacher.

SHARING THE WORKERS' PROBLEMS

It is said that the mother eagle induces her young to fly by throwing them out of the nest at the appropriate time. This may be a good method of teaching eagles to fly, but when applied to teaching Sunday School teachers to teach it is a very poor method. The teacher who is plunged into the work of teaching a class and then allowed to shift for himself without guidance or assistance will do one of three things: (1) he will get discouraged during the first few weeks and quit; (2) he will hark back to the methods used with him when he was a child in the Sunday School; or (3) he will, by his own effort, think his way through to effective ways of working. The third of these is the least likely to happen.

When a worker has taken up the duties of his office, the contacts between him and the general superintendent or the department principal should be many and frequent. Again and again must the supervisor seek contacts with his new workers in order to find out how their work is progressing. He should not depend on the new workers to come to him with their problems. Often they themselves are least conscious of their most serious problems.

In the fall when Ella Blackburn began teaching in the Primary Department, the school had just adopted a new system of lessons. The older teachers, as well as the new teachers, were confused by the materials which were handed to them. This gave the superintendent an opportunity to interpret for them the purpose of these new materials. In several meetings with the group of Primary teachers he gave them the most effective course in materials of teaching that they had ever had. It was not called teacher-training. It grew out of a vital need. Yet it was very effective teacher-training. Nor did this superintendent depend only on group meetings. During such time as he found available he interviewed individual teachers and visited their classes in order to determine whether they had really caught the spirit and purpose of the lesson materials which were in use.

The most frequent problems sensed by teachers in the Sunday School are those concerned with discipline. Usually, however, the difficulty is not so much with bad boys or unruly girls as with the teacher himself. The superintendent will need to make a study of the class in which there seem to be problems of discipline. Perhaps all that is needed is to give the teacher a little help with his teaching method. This may so improve his work that problems of discipline will disappear. If, however, they still persist, then direct attention should be given to the matter of securing good order, for without good order no effective teaching can be done.

There are various ways of helping the teacher with his problems. Perhaps the most important step is that of discovering what the problems really are. The best way to do this is to visit the teacher and observe his work. So important is this phase of supervision that we shall defer the discussion and give the entire next chapter to it.

TRAINING WORKERS IN SERVICE

While it is true that whenever possible workers should be trained before they take up their duties, there is something in favor of training them while they are actually in the service. Much is made these days of centering education in life. A worker who is actually engaged in the duties of the Sunday School has constantly before him the practical problems which he is meeting. Moreover, most workers will probably not think of taking training for service until they are actually enlisted in teaching or some other task. If we define supervision as the improvement of teaching, then a superintendent is engaged in supervisory work when he is using to train his workers whatever means are at his disposal.

Much of what has already been said should be classed as training of workers. Giving a new worker a proper conception of his job, bringing him through a public installation service to see the seriousness of the task which he undertakes, helping him with problems as they arise—all these are avenues of training in the best sense of the term. In this section, however, we are thinking of the more formal means of training.

One of the most effective avenues of training is the teachers' meeting or workers' conference. Most Sunday Schools which hold such meetings at all spend their time discussing the problems of the school. Often business details are allowed to take so much time that the meeting has little educational value. Happily this situation is changing. More and more such details are left to smaller committees, and the meetings of the larger group are devoted to educational programs of one kind or another. The discussion of this type of training venture we shall postpone until a later chapter.

Another means of training workers is to secure their attendance at conferences, institutes, and conventions. Without question much progress in religious education has come about through conventions. Some have concluded that the day of mass conventions is over. If this be true, then we need to think of a more effective way for utilizing such short-term meetings. There are many things which may be accomplished through one- or two-day conventions and institutes which can never be accomplished through training schools because of the large percentage of workers who cannot be induced to enroll in long-term schools. A superintendent in Florida gathered up as many of his teachers as his automobile could carry and drove them forty miles to a conference which was being conducted by a staff member of the International Council of Religious Education. On the way they decided on the key questions which they would bring before this leader. This superintendent was practicing good supervision.

When we think of the better preparation of workers we are at once reminded of leadership-training classes or community training schools. Thousands of workers every year are taking part in such enterprises. Many more who are now ignoring such opportunities will take advantage of them when superintendents and pastors realize that it is a part of their task to encourage workers to take such training. Denominational and interdenominational summer schools offer another training opportunity. Young people's conferences and camps suggest a means of training young people to become future leaders in the church. Many churches have found it a good investment to pay a part or all of the expenses of students in summer schools and young people's camps because of the values which such students have brought back as a result of their experiences. For example, a superintendent came to the conviction that one of the younger teachers in the Junior Department possessed possibilities for development as a future leader for that department.

He secured an appropriation from the school treasury to pay the expenses of this teacher to a summer training school, where she might take specific training in Junior work under the guidance of an expert. This was good supervision.

Observation of good teaching is another avenue of improvement. The superintendent should plan to make it possible for his teachers to see good work being done. This may be accomplished through encouraging workers to visit public-school teachers, or good teachers in the local Sunday School or some neighboring Sunday School, and through demonstration teaching. Often a teacher may be sent to observe another teacher who excels in a particular phase of teaching, such as story-telling or leading a discussion. Such specific reference to aspects of the teaching process will make the observation more effective and will make it easier to find good models.

The local church should also consider carefully the opportunities for training for leadership in college departments of religious education. From practically every church young people are going to college each year. All too often they come back at the end of the four-year course no more capable of taking positions of leadership than when they went away, and often much less inclined to do so. A bit of guidance when they first depart for college may yield rich fruit in consecrated leadership when they return to the local church.

Without doubt many a superintendent who reads these lines will say, at one point or another, "I could not do that." And perhaps he is right. Different superintendents will be able to do different things well. But, above everything else, this task is too important to be bungled by unskilled hands. In the list of suggestions which have been made there are surely many things which every superintendent can do, and is in fact now doing. Let him seize upon the things which he can best carry out in his own school. Let him move into new fields of supervision as he becomes able. Let him share with others the things which they may be able to do better than he. Thus, through coöperative effort, any Sunday School may move toward the enlistment and training of a more effective group of workers.

CHAPTER IV

VISITING THE TEACHER AT WORK

In this chapter the word "teacher" is used to designate anyone who deals with pupils as a leader in the program of religious education. He may be a class teacher, a worship leader, or a director of recreational activities. The word "supervisor" is used to designate the superintendent, the department principal, or anyone else who may be doing the work of supervision.

A young girl who was a member of a training class was asked to assume responsibility for teaching a class of Junior boys and girls. After talking the matter over with the superintendent she agreed to attempt the work if the superintendent would help her. The superintendent took her at her word. After she had had an opportunity to work with her class for a few Sundays he said to her: "I am going to do what I can to help you. Suppose I visit your class next Sunday and see what suggestions I can make."

"Oh, that would just scare me to death," she answered.

After talking it over, however, she agreed that she could think of him as a helper and not as a critic and that she would be willing to teach in his presence. On the day of his visit the superintendent arrived at the opening of the class and stayed throughout the period. After a casual glance or two the pupils seemed entirely to ignore his presence.

Following this visit he made an appointment with the teacher to discuss her work. The appointment was scheduled for the middle of the week so that both might have an opportunity to see the session in the objective light which comes from being removed from it by a day or two. Out of the discussion grew plans for the teacher's use of the blackboard, for a more orderly procedure in handling materials for use in the class, for a greater freedom on the part of the teacher in the use of the lesson materials, and for a larger participation of pupils in the work of the class.

The most effective way to better teaching is to improve the teachers. The chief concern of the supervisor must therefore be *teacher growth*. The workers of the school may be thought of as the superintendent's class. Just as it is each teacher's duty to produce growth in Christian living, so it is the supervisor's duty to produce growth in teaching ability. Just as the teacher must know the life situations of his pupils if he is to lead them into richer and more effective experience, so the supervisor must know the teaching and leadership situations of his workers if he is to lead them into a more effective teaching experience. Training for teaching will be most effective and practical when it is based on the actual problems and needs of the teacher.

The best way for the supervisor to learn the actual problems and situations which his workers are facing is to observe them at their work.

A CASE IN DIAGNOSIS

This first step toward helping the teacher improve his work may be called *diagnosis*. A teacher is having difficulty with his class, and the superintendent has been asked to lend a hand. He may get the teacher's version of the difficulty, but if he is wise he will go himself to see the "patient." Arriving in the class, he will make a careful observation of the work and try to locate the cause of the difficulty. He may go beyond the class session and inquire into particulars about pupils and teacher; that is, he makes a "case study." Upon the basis of all the facts he can learn he makes his suggestions for improvement; that is, he "prescribes" his remedy.

Can a chorus of superintendents be heard saying, "But I couldn't do that!"? It must be admitted that the task is difficult. It is difficult because most superintendents feel that they do not know so much about teaching as do the teachers. It is difficult also because there is an unfortunate attitude of mind on the part of most workers which would lead them to resent such suggestions.

It may be impossible for many superintendents to do anything of this sort. Yet there are some superintendents who could give a large amount of help to their teachers through this method. All should strive to develop a better attitude on the part of teachers toward supervisory suggestions. Superintendents who do not feel competent to discharge this duty will do well to enlist others who can do it. Perhaps the department principals can help their teachers. Perhaps one or more competent persons can be found who may be relieved from teaching duty and used as "helping teachers." The work of supervision is so important that, if at all possible, some provision should be made for it.

PREPARATION FOR THE VISIT

It is highly important that the proper attitude be developed between the supervisor and teacher. This requires that preparation be made for the visit. It is desirable that the visit be made on the invitation of the teacher. Experience has taught the writer, however, that teachers who need help most are the least likely to ask for it. It may require weeks and months of work and fellowship to develop an attitude of acceptance of the supervisor as a helping teacher, yet the development of this attitude is essential. Unless the supervisor can come with the consent of the teacher it is doubtful whether the visit will have much value.

It should be emphasized also that supervising is a two-way process. The supervisor and the teacher are coworkers in a common task. Together they must seek to improve the process of teaching. Again the analogy between the work of the supervisor and the work of the teacher is seen. Just as the teacher is sharing with his pupils in discovering Christian outcomes in life situations, so the supervisor is sharing with the teacher the problems involved in developing good teaching method.

Particular attention should be given to new teachers. It is not fair to expect a new worker to undertake a task as difficult as teaching religion and then leave him entirely to his own devices. A long forward step toward developing the right attitude between teacher and supervisor will have been taken if, when a teacher is appointed, it is understood that the supervisor will assist him in getting started.

In so far as possible the supervisor should see a normal session of the department, class, or group. Hence some educators recommend that the supervisor should come unannounced. With most Sunday School workers, however, the sudden appearance of the supervisor would probably upset the best of plans. On the whole, it will probably be better for the teacher and supervisor to have a conference preceding the visit. In this conference they should arrive at an understanding of what they hope to accomplish. The teacher should state clearly what he is expecting to do during the session in question. A written lesson plan will be helpful as a basis of discussion. The teacher might also state his greatest difficulty, and any point on which he is hoping for help from the supervisor. The supervisor on his part should make clear what the teacher may expect of him. This should develop the free attitude which will make supervisor and teacher of one mind and purpose when the visit is made.

It is of value for the supervisor, before he visits a group, to know something about the pupils. If the school has a good system of permanent records, it will be well for him to examine the records of the pupils in the group which he is to visit. This is not an impossible task in the ordinary small class. It is desirable also for the supervisor to have had previous contacts with the pupils so that when he comes into the group his presence will be taken as a matter of course.

THE VISIT

It is important that the supervisor come, quietly and unobtrusively, at the very beginning of the session. It is important that he stay through the entire session. Most class and department sessions in the Sunday School are so brief that unless the whole period can be observed it is not possible to get a true picture of the work of the teacher.

During his presence in the room it is important that the supervisor be as inconspicuous as possible, so that he will not distract attention from the main business of the class. For this reason, a position in the back of the room may be best. On the other hand, it is easier for him to observe the pupils if he can see their faces, and let it be remembered that the pupils are the most important persons to observe. Yet if the supervisor takes his position at the front of the room he is apt to cause a division of interest between himself and the teacher. A satisfactory compromise is a position far enough to one side to avoid distracting the attention of the pupils and yet far enough forward to offer a fair opportunity for observing the children.

What is the supervisor to do during his visit in the room? Let it be remembered that he is to *observe*, and not to assist. This should be made clear to the teacher beforehand. Let the supervisor be an interested observer! As the work proceeds let him make mental notes of points which may be discussed with the teacher later. Perhaps he may also make written notes, but care should be taken not to disturb the teacher.

What shall the supervisor observe? A general visit without attention to specific things will not be of great value. In a pamphlet entitled "How to Judge a Beginners Department," [1] Miss Frances Weld Danielson makes the suggestion that the thing to observe first is not the room, or the equipment, or the teacher, but the children. The attitude of the children is the best guide to discovering the effective-

---

[1] Danielson, Frances Weld, "How to Judge a Beginners Department." Congregational Education Society, Boston. 1921.

ness of the work. Therefore note first: *Are the children interested?* If not, discover the reason. Is it physical discomfort? Is it because the pupils are poorly graded? Is it because of the personality of the teacher? Is it because the lesson material is not appropriate? Is it because the teaching is poor? The answer to each of these questions suggests the help which should be given to the teacher in improving the work. If, on the other hand, the attitude of the pupils is entirely satisfactory, then the visitor should ask further: *What are they getting?* Are they getting a religious interpretation of life? gaining fruitful knowledge? developing right attitudes and high ideals? acquiring right habits of conduct? The answers to these questions will suggest the points at which the teacher needs help.

It would be helpful for the supervisor to have a check list before him indicating some of the more important items which he desires to observe. In different groups he may desire to lay stress upon different items in the list. Such a check list will make the observation which he is making more specific, and will help him to see many things which otherwise might be overlooked. Excellent check lists which have been prepared for public-school supervisors will be found in "The Supervision of Instruction" [2] by Barr and Burton, pages 153, 157. The following list

[2] Barr, A. S., and Burton, W. H., "The Supervision of Instruction." D. Appleton and Company, New York, 1926.

is introduced as an illustration of what may be useful to Sunday School superintendents.

A LIST OF QUESTIONS TO AID IN THE OBSERVATION OF TEACHING

I. THE PUPILS:

1. Do they enter into the work with evident enjoyment?
2. Is the work of the class "serious business" for them?
3. Do they have a purpose in what they do?
4. Do they participate as though the session were their very own?
5. Are they orderly; that is, are their activities centered on the work of the class?
6. Are they grouped advantageously for work?
7. Are they comfortable, that is, properly seated with hats and coats removed?

II. THE TEACHER:

1. Is he natural and thoroughly at home in the group?
2. Does he use his voice to the best advantage?
3. Does he have a purpose and plan for the session? Is his plan flexible enough to provide for the pupils' interests and needs as revealed in the work of the class?
4. Does he handle problems of discipline skillfully?
5. Does he allow for pupil initiative, purposing, and planning? Are contributions of the pupils used in developing the lesson, or are they ignored or treated as interruptions?
6. Does he guide the pupils skillfully, both with reference to the oral suggestions he makes and in the textbook and reference-book assignments?
7. Does he use method skillfully: tell a story well, ask questions skillfully, guide discussion helpfully, and so forth?
8. Does he draw out his pupils skillfully, so that all may share in the work of the group?
9. Does he attempt to check up his results to determine whether the pupils are actually learning?
10. Does he show evidence of being well prepared?

III. THE WORK:

1. Is it worth while? Does it touch the life situations and needs of the pupils?
2. Is it religious? Does it help to give a religious interpretation of life?
3. Is it Christian? Are problems in living decided in a Christian way?
4. Is it constructive? Does it result in the giving of fruitful knowledge, the building of right attitudes, and the establishment of Christian habits?
5. Does it "lead on"? Is there provision for new study and investigation (assignment)?
6. Does it enlist the interest and attention of every pupil and help him to make a constructive contribution to the whole group?
7. Does good order prevail? Is there good system in passing to and from the room, distributing pencils, paper, and other supplies?

IV. THE ROOM:

1. Is it comfortably heated, adequately lighted, and properly ventilated?
2. Is it of proper size (fifteen square feet per pupil)?
3. Is the room attractively arranged and decorated, comparing favorably with the standards prevailing in the homes of these pupils?
4. Is the furniture adequate; are seats of the right height, with sufficient work space for each pupil?
5. Is the seating of the pupils arranged to the best advantage with reference to light, space, entrance, distractions, and so forth?
6. Is the room clean and orderly?

THE CONFERENCE FOLLOWING THE VISIT OF THE SUPERVISOR

It is important that, following a visit to a department, class, or group, the supervisor shall have an unhurried conference with the leader whose work has been observed. No matter what the results of the observation may be the supervisor owes it to the leader to talk over with him his impressions of the visit.

1. WHEN SHOULD SUCH A CONFERENCE BE HELD? It should certainly not be held immediately after the class. Usually there is no time then for a deliberate conference. More than likely the supervisor has not yet organized his ideas for proper discussion. Certainly the teacher, if he has given himself completely to his task, is in no frame of mind to discuss the session immediately. It is much better to make an appointment for a conference later in the week when ample time may be devoted to it to permit adequate discussion. Let the supervisor remember that this is his supreme opportunity for improving the work of the teacher.

2. WHAT SHALL BE DONE IN SUCH A CONFERENCE? It should be businesslike and to the point. General conversation alone will not bring about improvement, though there should be a few generalities to put the teacher at ease. There are three things which the supervisor should accomplish in this conference:

a. He should commend that which is praiseworthy in the teacher's work. Few teachers are so poor that there are not some aspects of their work which really deserve commendation. The teacher should be made to feel that he is achieving a measure of success and that his work is appreciated, but praise should not be so overdone that it loses its effectiveness.

b. He should condemn whatever might be classed as bad practice. Few teachers are so perfect that there are not some things which can be bettered. Discriminating evaluation is necessary if improvement in teaching is to result.

c. He should make suggestions for improvement. This is the most important aspect of the conference. The visit and conference have been of very little value if as a result thereof the teacher does not go back to the task with a better conception of what he must do and how it may best be done.

The conference must be *educational*. It should help the teacher to grow. It should help him to think through his whole task. Often it is better for the supervisor to ask questions which require the teacher to think his work through for himself than to give direct suggestions. The teacher should be helped to see the relationship between the work he is doing and the general principles of education which he has learned in his training. The discussion should be as objective as possible. It should be on the basis of generally recognized principles, with the two persons who are talking it over effaced as far as possible from consideration. Reading references may be cited which will help the teacher in mastering a certain difficulty. This is far better than attempting to convey orally ideas from a background in educational literature which might offer guidance. There should be an atmosphere of experimentation in which teacher and

5

supervisor together work out problems for which no dogmatic solution can be given.

Above all things the supervisor should be sensible and tactful in such a conference. It is not necessary to reveal to a teacher in one conference all that he should know. It is not necessary to point out all that is wrong with a class or department session. The teacher should be permitted to feel the joy of success in mastering step by step the improvements which are agreed upon coöperatively. It is not necessary to criticize bluntly. The English language possesses many words which may be used in saying with tact that which in its lowest terms would sound very harsh.

Finally, the supervisor should not assume that one visit and conference is sufficient to improve the work of a teacher. The supervisory process should be continuous. After a certain interval of time other visits should be made to see if there has been improvement. It is better to give thoroughgoing attention to the improvement of a few workers than to visit hastily many workers without taking adequate time to make the visits effective.

A program of class and department visits will unquestionably reveal many problems which are faced by more than one worker. These may well form the basis for group conferences. Often a program for the workers' conference may be effectively arranged around questions which have arisen in the course of class visits. Undoubtedly the group conference provides a way of bringing before the workers criticism of present practices and suggestions for improvement without making the matter too personal.

CHAPTER V

THE WORKERS' CONFERENCE

In this chapter the workers' conference as a means to Sunday School improvement will be considered, and various ways will be discussed by which the conference may be made most effective. The workers' conference is a meeting of the working staff of the school. Almost every Sunday School holds some sort of meeting of its teachers and officers, even though it be only once a year. Few schools, however, have experienced the great value which may result from such conferences conducted on an educational basis.

WHY SOME FAIL

In many cases the teachers' or workers' conference does nothing more than discuss the details of the business administration of the school. Few workers are interested in these details. The major part of administrative management should be carried by the executive chosen for this purpose, or by a smaller group. The usual result of making the workers' conference a meeting for the consideration of business is that few of the workers participate with interest, and consequently after a time they fail to attend.

Some schools, having caught a vision of how the workers' conference may be vitalized through making it serve as a training agency for the workers, have gone to the other extreme of making it only a lecture or a lesson. While this may hold the interest for a time, the chances are great that such a lecture will be so far removed from the interests of the school or from the understanding of the majority of the workers that little success will be realized.

A PRACTICAL EDUCATIONAL VENTURE

What, then, shall be done with the workers' conference? The best answer will be found if the purposes inherent in the two approaches suggested are combined. An effective workers' conference must be more than a meeting to conduct business. It must also be more than a teacher training class.

Let us look for a moment at a modern theory of education to see how the workers' conference fits into its doctrine. Much is said to-day about making education life-centered or child-centered. Education for teachers, then, should also be life-centered. The purpose in training teachers is to make them more effective in the work of the Sunday School. Training enterprises should, therefore, center in the life experience of teachers, that is, in their *teaching* experience.

What better way of doing this is there than to let the workers' conference deal with such great problems of religious teaching as require careful study and discussion? This is more worth while than spending an evening in deciding whether or not free lemonade shall be served at the Sunday School picnic. It is more worth while than hearing a lecture on the project method. It is education which grows out of real life situations and, if effective, enters the very processes of the work which the teachers are doing.

An example will serve to illustrate this point. The Committee on Religious Education of a certain school had discussed for some time the problem of closer relationship between school and home. It was proposed that quarterly report cards covering the work of the pupils should be sent to the homes. Such a plan involves more than administrative detail for it goes to the very heart of the teacher's work. A meeting of the workers' conference of this school was therefore devoted to a presentation of the proposed plan and a discussion both of its desirability and of the method of putting it into effect. The result of this evening's work was not simply to make the system of pupil reports a success but, what is more important, to give the teachers a new insight into the seriousness of the work in which they were engaged and their responsibility toward parents and children for the faithful discharge of the task undertaken.

SOURCES OF TOPICS

Where shall the superintendent get the problems which may most effectively be used for his workers' conferences?

The Workers' Conference

The answer is perfectly simple. *They must grow out of the very life of the school.* The superintendent must make a constant study of his school and its needs. He will find that there are more than enough problems to keep the workers' conference busy for a year.

Just as in the teaching of pupils life situations are used to make it vital, so the most important situations which arise out of the teaching process should form the basis for teacher-training through the workers' conference. Some one may suggest that this is a hand-to-mouth process and that it will not permit the carrying out of the admirable plan which some Sunday Schools have of listing their topics for a year in advance. Yet this need not be the case. The superintendent's study of his school one year may well serve as a background for the listing of topics for the following year. However, it is not essential that topics be listed for twelve months in advance. The activity of the workers' conference becomes more vital if the selection of the problems is more closely related to their emergence in the life of the school.

What are some of the problems that might arise in the work of Sunday Schools as they exist, which might well be treated in a workers' conference? A few illustrations will serve to send the mind of any superintendent exploring among the problems of his own local situation.

1. The beginning of the school year is the time when a large percentage of new teachers are assigned their duties. Moreover, teachers who have formerly served are assigned new classes and possibly new lesson materials. It would seem, therefore, that the first workers' conference might well be held before the actual opening of the new year, and that it might profitably be devoted to a presentation and discussion of some of the fundamental principles on which the work of the school should be based. What is to be accomplished? What is the purpose of the existing organization? What kind of lessons are being used? What are some of the difficult features about the lessons? What is expected of a teacher by the Sunday School? These and other problems need frank discussion in order that a wholesome point of view may be early developed.

2. It may be that a Sunday School is dissatisfied with its record system and with its handling of pupil personnel. Perhaps a new system of records is to be introduced. This situation should serve as an occasion for careful discussion of pupil management. When is a pupil enrolled? How is this school securing new pupils? How successfully is it holding its pupils? How many of the pupils who enroll in this school become permanently connected with the church and its work? Are these facts definitely known? How promptly do the pupils attend the

Sunday School? What items covering the work of pupils should be recorded permanently in the records of the school? If a new system of records is being adopted, what are its major features? What must the teacher do in order to keep such records properly? What must the department principal do? Other similar problems will present themselves in the consideration of this topic.

3. The curriculum of the school is an ever-present problem which requires consideration and interpretation if teachers are to do their best work. In most schools the curriculum problem is tied up very closely with the lessons in use, though the word curriculum, as used to-day, covers other activities besides the study of lessons. Many Sunday Schools are adopting new lessons year by year. Most teachers accept the materials handed them and use them blindly, with little understanding of what is to be accomplished. Many teachers do not even read the introductory sections of teachers' quarterlies which are so essential to an understanding of the thing which the lesson writer is hoping will be accomplished. A part of the workers' conference might well be taken for a discussion of the underlying principles of lesson selection, followed by specific application of such principles to the materials selected by this school.

4. Sometimes a special interest arises which should be interpreted to the entire working group. Thus in

one Sunday School a special emphasis was to be placed on Bible geography and a young woman was engaged to serve as helping teacher in this field. To launch this enterprise, a session of the workers' conference was devoted to a presentation of the important place of Bible geography in the teaching of religion. Following that presentation, each worker made a relief map of Palestine under the guidance of the special teacher of geography. This same school at another time inaugurated a program placing special emphasis on missionary education. This was carried out under the direction of the professor of missions in a seminary located in the same city. An entire meeting of the workers' conference was turned over to him for discussion with the workers of the plans which he was proposing for the entire school for a period of three months.

5. A Committee on Religious Education came to the conclusion that the next most important step in the improvement of the work of the school would be a closer relationship between parents and teachers. A discussion of the important place of the home in the Christian nurture of boys and girls was followed by a decision on the part of the workers' conference to hold a parent-teacher supper, which might make an opportunity for the school to interpret its work to the parents and for parents and teachers to become better acquainted. Both the discussion of the problem and the sharing in the parent-

teacher supper were of unusual educative value for the workers of this school.

6. The adoption of the International Standard for the Church School provided one school with a series of topics for its workers' conferences. The plan followed was that of careful study of the entire Church School by means of this standard. This involved a series of workers' conference meetings, lasting throughout the major part of a year. Throughout the study the school itself was made the subject of study and the Standard served merely as a guide in uncovering the problems of the school and suggesting ways of improvement.

7. An interesting feature for a workers' conference is to have several workers report orally on the most interesting educational articles or books which they have read during the month. Several workers should be appointed in advance to make such reports. The educational value will be increased if articles are assigned to these reporters, especially if they are chosen with regard to the problems of the individuals to whom they are assigned.

8. If an excursion has been made to another Sunday School, an interesting program may be built up around the reports of the visitors. The discussion should not simply deal with a critical evaluation of what has been seen but should also raise sharply the question of what new ideas for the work of the home school may be gleaned from the visit.

LIMITATIONS OF THE WORKERS' CONFERENCE

After a due evaluation of the importance of the workers' conference in the improvement of teaching in the local church has been made, it should in all fairness be added that there are limitations to what the workers' conference can accomplish.

While the conference may enlist a larger percentage of the workers than is usually available for courses in leadership training, it must be recognized that even if the conference meets regularly once a month, it will take an entire year to equal one unit in leadership training. Moreover, when such a conference meets but once each month it is almost impossible to carry out a continuous program. Those who have tried to use a unit of the leadership curriculum in the course of a year of workers' conferences have discovered that there is not sufficient continuity to make the plan effective.

The workers' conference should not be regarded as a final goal but rather as an important step toward the realization of teacher improvement, and, in turn, toward more intensive training work on the part of many of the workers.

ADMINISTRATIVE ASPECTS

This brief discussion is intended to deal with the educational aspect of the workers' conference rather than with its administrative problems. Perhaps just a word should be said about the latter. The writer has found that monthly conferences through ten months of the year are most effective in the schools which he has served. He has found also that the most effective way of securing attendance is through a supper meeting followed by a program which terminates not later than nine o'clock.

The program for the workers' conference may be set up in a variety of ways, of which the following is typical:

6.30 Supper
7.00 Fellowship singing, toasts, or other forms of entertainment
7.15 Worship (led by one of the teachers)
7.30 Address by a visiting speaker
8.00 Discussion of address
8.15 Reports on reading
8.30 Announcements and other business
8.50 Brief departmental conclaves for announcements, arrangements for departmental conferences, and so forth
9.00 Adjournment

The plan of holding a supper meeting has the advantages of providing an opportunity for fellowship and of making a longer period available without holding the meeting unduly long. The fellowship phase of the conference should not be overlooked, for it is often the only opportunity which workers have to get acquainted with one another. The worship phase of the conference also should not be overlooked, for what better purpose can be found for engaging in common worship than the facing of a great common task like the teaching of religion?

Securing the regular attendance of the workers is always a problem. It requires constant effort. A first approach to regular attendance should be made by impressing upon every teacher when he is appointed to a teaching position that attendance at the workers' conferences is involved in his acceptance, just as much as attendance at the Sunday School hour. A record of attendance at the workers' conference should be kept. Responsibility should be laid upon department heads to secure the attendance of the teachers in each department. A friendly rivalry among departments to see which can secure the best attendance may even be justified. Special participation on the part of whole departments in the activities of the workers' conference meeting is helpful in developing department solidarity. The telephone, the typewriter, and personal contact must be used from month to month in stimulating attendance. Most of all, the meetings themselves must be made so attractive that he who must be absent feels a sense of loss so keenly that he will make every effort to keep that one evening in the month free for the work of the Sunday School. It is a worthy ideal to make the meeting of the workers' conference the happiest evening of the month in the activities of the church.

We have defined the membership of the workers' conference as consisting of the working staff of the Sunday School. This should be interpreted to mean every one who has a part in the entire teaching work of the church, whether it be the Sunday School, Vacation School, Home Department, Society, or other agency. Occasion should be made frequently to invite others who may be prospective workers. Membership in the group should be a privilege, generously extended to those who are willing to qualify.

Chapter VI

IMPROVING THE PROGRAM OF WORK

The Sunday School exists for the pupil, and not the pupil for the Sunday School. The only thing which ultimately matters is what happens in the life of the pupil. It is that the child may learn to live the Christian life that the school of religion is established. The superintendent's chief interest and persistent care must be that every pupil in his school may grow in the Christian way of life.

The expression "program of work" is meant to cover the various activities in which pupils engage because they are members of the Sunday School. These activities may be carried out as work in the school, or they may represent outside activities which the school is stimulating, guiding, and enriching. They may include study and reading, worship, service, helpfulness in the work of the school, offerings, listening to stories and talks, giving talks or telling stories, engaging in constructive work. The word "curriculum" is sometimes used to indicate these various activities in which pupils engage. The word is also used to mean textbooks and materials, but this is too narrow an interpretation. The curriculum should be thought of as *including* lesson materials.

THE TEACHER AND THE CURRICULUM

"Why do you have your pupils go through this particular routine of worship and instruction? Why did you teach this particular lesson rather than some other?" a Sunday School teacher was asked. She hesitated, became confused, and finally said, "I don't know, unless it is because that is the way everybody does in Sunday School." Is this sufficient reason for an hour of varied activity?

Teachers need to see clearly the purpose of their work. The activities of the school must be used as tools in the accomplishment of that purpose. Only when this attitude is taken will the curriculum have life and power.

How does growth in Christian living come about? The program of work which is carried out in the school will depend on the answer to this question. If it is through knowledge of the Bible, the effective teaching of the Bible must be the school's chief concern. If it is through worship, the experience of worship must be the chief concern. If it is through service for others, a program of service activities must occupy the center of attention. A school which understands its task will be lifted above the confusion of many unrelated activities and will do only those things which minister directly to helping pupils in learning to live the Christian life.

The problem of how best to bring about growth in Christian character is one which requires much further study and experimentation. It is clear, however, that people learn to live by *living*. A Sunday School must not limit its work to a study about life, but must constitute an experience in living, under the guidance of Christian teaching. Knowledge is an important element in learning to live. It must not be given a place of central concern, as is usually the case, but must be made to minister to the needs of life. This is what is meant by making the school *life*-centered.

The emphasis on life needs has been responsible for very significant changes in the work of Sunday Schools in recent years. Effort is being made to help the pupil to see the religious significance of his everyday living and to help him to develop the ideals and habits necessary in meeting situations in a Christian way. The life of the school itself is looked upon as a venture in Christian living, in which pupils may share with one another and with their teachers in doing Christlike deeds. The emphasis is on *experience* in living rather than on knowledge to be acquired.

VARIED ACTIVITIES IN THE CURRICULUM

When life needs are to be met it becomes obvious that many types of activities may be used to achieve the desired result in Christian living. The thing the pupil is made to do must always be understood in terms of the quality of Christian living to be brought about.

The various phases into which the curriculum may be divided are given by the International Standards in Religious Education as follows:

1. WORSHIP. The experience of vital fellowship with God. This is a unique contribution of the Sunday School. Through worship the whole of the pupil's life should be lifted to the consciousness of his relation to God.

2. SERVICE. The experience of outgoing fellowship with and for others. Through service activities the pupil may be led to learn the Christian way of life by actually doing the works of the Kingdom.

3. RECREATION. The experience of living together with other pupils and with teachers in the interest of wholesome enjoyment and under Christian guidance. Recreation, to be worthy of a place in the Sunday School curriculum, must minister definitely to learning to live the Christian life. Leisure-time activities are very potent in character growth.

4. STUDY. The experience of seeking light in living the life of to-day according to the example and teaching of Jesus. Study in this sense includes projects, discussion, investigation, reading, observation trips, dramatic activities, and actual enterprises in Christian living.

In actual practice these various phases of the curriculum intermingle. Worship involves study, and true study involves worship. Constructive service may grow out of study, and will require much study while it is in process. And certainly service should be rendered in the spirit of worship.

THE SUPERINTENDENT AND THE CURRICULUM

It may in fairness be said that the superintendent has only an indirect relation to the curriculum. It is the teachers and department leaders who have the direct contacts with the pupils. It must be remembered, however, that the superintendent is also a supervisor, and that he must be vitally concerned in what pupils are learning because this represents the product for which the school exists. Unless the most fruitful activities are being carried out, the desired product in Christian character will not be forthcoming. It would seem, then, that the superintendent must be definitely aware of and concerned in what is going on in every class and every department. He should make it an important part of his business to help every teacher to develop the most fruitful curriculum for his group.

The superintendent must help his teachers to understand how character changes are brought about. He must lead them to see the significance of the activities of the school, and to test the effectiveness of these activities in pupil conduct. To a great many teachers their work means little more than getting the pupils to give intelligent answers to questions based on the text. To all too many it means nothing more than keeping the pupils interested for the period of the class session, no matter by what. Unless these teachers can be led to see a vital relation between the work they are doing and the life interests and needs of their pupils, only meager results may be expected.

The superintendent must make sure that the curriculum provides a varied experience. It is so easy to follow a stereotyped program that constant vigilance must be practiced to make sure that the curriculum of religious education adequately represents the needs of life. Here is a superintendent who feels that temperance education has been too much neglected in recent years and that as a consequence a great area of life experience is being untouched by religious education. He is casting about for program material which may be used in building departmental worship programs around this theme. Here is another superintendent who feels that the casual reference to missions in the regular course of lessons is not sufficient to give the pupils in his school a broad concept of the meaning of world friendship. He organizes an extensive program of missionary education which brings a vital missionary emphasis not only into the worship programs and class discussions but also into the whole church life for a period of weeks. Here is a third superintendent who feels that the social contacts of pupils with one another and with their teachers is not sufficiently free and

frequent to promote the best working together on
Sundays. He introduces a plan whereby the leaders
in every department are encouraged to arrange for
Christmas parties during the holiday season. Here
is a fourth superintendent who feels the need of
wholesome contacts between his pupils and persons
of other races. He arranges for a special Sunday
on which his school entertains visitors from a colored
Sunday School in a near-by city. An opportunity
is given the visitors to contribute to the program.
These are a few illustrations of how fruitful emphases
may be given to the curriculum through proper
supervision.

The superintendent must so organize the curriculum of his Sunday School that the varied experiences form one unified whole in the lives of the pupils.
In a modern church program it is very easy to have
independent programs, often so unrelated as to result
in much duplication of effort and division of energy.
In building his curriculum the superintendent must
take account of the various educative influences and
facilities supplied by his church and utilize all to the
greatest possible extent. For example, the Inter-
mediate boys may be members of a church troop of
Boy Scouts. The curriculum of the Sunday School
should take definite account of the experience these
boys are having in their through-the-week activities.
Again, pupils attending the church service of worship are having a certain type of experience which

should not be ignored by those who are responsible for worship in the Sunday School.

What has been said concerning the relation of the superintendent to the curriculum indicates that the curriculum is broader than the work which is done in individual classes, and that the supervision of curriculum activities touches not only what teachers are doing in classes but also what is being done by leaders of worship and leaders of recreational and other activities. Herein lies the answer to the question, "In a completely departmentalized school, what is there left for the superintendent to do?" The superintendent has a far more important task than leading the general program of worship. He must see that every department has a satisfactory program of worship, and every class a satisfactory program of study and activities.

LESSON MATERIALS

In the above discussion the curriculum has been viewed from the standpoint of activities in which pupils engage and the resulting influence of such experience on character. In the minds of many people a curriculum is a set of lesson materials. In the older use of the term it is true that curriculum did mean lesson materials, but the broader meaning is now generally assumed. In any case, however, an effective curriculum will include materials for both pupil and teacher to be used in carrying forward the desirable activities.

When the matter of teaching materials is considered, a wider and a narrower use of this term may be recognized. In the wider sense teaching materials include not only the particular quarterly or textbook in use but also hymn books, pictures, Bibles, reference books, magazines, and so forth. In the narrower sense, teaching materials include the lesson books or quarterlies which form a part of the system of lessons which may be in use in the school. For the remainder of this section teaching materials will be considered in this narrower sense.

In recent years some marked changes have taken place in the teaching materials which are published for use in Sunday Schools. The older teaching materials consisted of certain Bible texts and other content texts. These constituted material to be learned by the pupil. The newer materials give more attention to directions to the teacher for initiating desirable activities and meeting life needs, and place text materials in a secondary position. We may recognize two types of material: *first*, method guides for both teacher and pupil, which aim to lead the work of the class into channels of fruitful activity; *second*, pupil's source materials through which the pupil may be guided in meeting the situations and needs of everyday life. The latter may be in the form of guidance to source materials in libraries, art galleries, current literature, and the general life of the community.

Looking at lesson materials from this standpoint we may distinguish four general classes.

1. IMPROVED UNIFORM LESSONS. The first product of the International Lesson Committee was in the form of uniform lessons, and the Committee is still continuing to furnish outlines for such uniform lessons in deference to a demand from the field for such materials, particularly for adult Bible classes. In no case would the present writer recommend the use of uniform lessons throughout the school.

2. GROUP GRADED LESSONS.[1] These lessons strike a halfway mark between uniform lessons and closely graded lessons. They are graded by age groups or departments. Thus, on a given Sunday, all Primary pupils will be using the same lesson, all Junior pupils the same lesson, and so on for each of the departments. The outlines for the group graded lessons are produced by a subcommittee of the Educational Commission of the International Council (formerly the International Lesson Committee) and are published by most of the denominations. The lessons are issued in inexpensive quarterly form and dated for each Sunday.

3. CLOSELY GRADED LESSONS. Materials under this general classification provide a different course

---

[1] By some denominations these are designated DEPARTMENTAL GRADED LESSONS. In the Presbyterian Church in the United States of America these Departmental Lessons have been expanded into AGE GROUP PROGRAMS, which provide materials for all departments and activities in the Church School.

for each year in the Sunday School. In the early development of this type of material the International Lesson Committee outlined a system of closely graded lessons, and these when published by the several denominations bore the name "The International Graded Series." More recently the production of closely graded lessons has been taken over by the denominations, working individually or in groups. There is no longer a so-called International Graded Series. Several series of graded lessons are now available. In addition to the closely graded lessons published by denominational houses there are also several systems published by independent publishers.

4. INDEPENDENT MATERIALS. This classification includes the increasing number of courses which are appearing at various age levels but which are not built into systems for the entire Sunday School. Both denominational publishers and independent publishers have issued materials of this sort. Some of the more advanced materials, judged by the newer curriculum theories, are to be found in this classification.

Obviously, any Sunday School which plans to have a systematic and integrated curriculum of religious education must exercise some care in the selection of lesson materials. One of the major functions of the superintendent, therefore, is his responsibility, in coöperation with his workers and with the board of religious education, for the selection of teaching materials.

Not only the need for a systematic plan and program should be emphasized, but also the need for giving each leader and his group the materials which are best fitted to meet their needs. Many schools follow the practice of using throughout the school one or another of the available systems of lessons. Others, and perhaps those with more competent executive leadership, feel free to build up what may be called an "eclectic" system of lessons through considering the available materials for each grade and selecting that which is best for that grade. When the latter plan is followed it is, nevertheless, a good practice to use as an outline or framework one of the complete systems of lessons and substitute other materials in the course wherever such substitution seems desirable. The system of lessons thus gives an outline which will help to avoid duplication and the overlooking of certain essential areas.

In addition to carrying the responsibility for selecting the lesson materials to be used, the superintendent must also assume responsibility for having the materials properly *installed*. In other words, the teacher who is to use the lesson materials must know what they are intended to accomplish, and why a particular course has been chosen rather than some other. For this reason it is a good plan for the teacher to be a party to the choice of materials.

MEETING THE COST

As Sunday Schools are launching out in the use of the newer type of lesson materials, many of them are finding that the expense is considerably greater than that to which they have been accustomed. If, for example, an entire Junior Department should be using a course which requires each pupil to have a bound textbook, the initial cost will be almost one dollar per pupil. Let it be granted that too little has been spent on Sunday Schools in the past; nevertheless, the purchase of this more expensive type of material constitutes a problem for the school in which the money is not available.

Two suggestions may be made, growing out of the writer's own experience. First, such textbooks may be purchased by the school and lent to the pupils for the year. The following year a different group of pupils will be using the same books, thus avoiding a new outlay for lesson materials that year. If it may be assumed that a textbook will be good for three years, the actual cost per year will be less than is the case when the cheaper kind of pamphlet material is given outright to the pupil. Second, the pupil may be permitted to buy the textbooks by paying one half of the cost, the Sunday School bearing the other half. In this way the cost will be no greater than for the usual type of pamphlet material and the pupil will have a neatly bound book for his use, which he may treasure in his library for years to come. Most pupils of the ages for which such books are practical are willing to share the expense in this way. A combination of these two plans would be that of making the matter optional with the pupil as to whether he will buy a book or receive it as a loan from the Sunday School.

In this discussion on textbooks it is not intended to imply that cloth-bound books are in every case better than the cheaper pamphlet material. In fact, some of the latter type of materials now available may, in many cases, be found to be superior in meeting the needs of a particular group.

GENERAL WORKING MATERIALS

Finally, in his work in relation to the curriculum, the superintendent must give careful thought to adequately supplying each teacher and officer with working materials. This means that materials must be selected and ordered early enough to allow the teacher to become thoroughly familiar with a course before beginning to teach it. It means that an ample supply of material must be provided, that each pupil must be properly supplied, and that there shall be a minimum of waste. It means that there must be a system of filing whereby teachers' books which can be used year after year are properly kept, and whereby any surplus material may be held over for the following year. The amount of loss which is involved in most Sunday Schools at just this point would help to pay for improvement in equipment and other needs of the school. It means further that workers must be supplied with such supplemental materials as may be needed for doing the most effective work. No teacher should be handicapped because of lack of reference books and other materials.

It will not be out of place to add that the supply department of the Sunday School should be so well organized that each teacher may easily and quickly secure the materials necessary, and that good business methods will prevail throughout. Every bill which is to be paid by the Sunday School should cover only such orders as have been approved by a responsible officer.

When we have discussed the relation of the superintendent to the curriculum we have touched the very heart of his problem. The one thing which matters most is what is happening to the pupils when the Sunday School is at work. Competent teachers, adequate housing and equipment, systems of records, and so forth, while very important in themselves, are nevertheless but instrumental to the creation of the best possible curriculum.

Chapter VII

SCHOOL IMPROVEMENT THROUGH RECORDS AND REPORTS

Whether we look at his work from the angle of organization, administration, or supervision, we see that the superintendent must have accurate records available if he is to do his best.

The keeping of records in most Sunday Schools is like so many of the things we do in life—it was started with a purpose in view, but that purpose has long since vanished while the activity still goes on. Most schools would find it difficult to give an adequate answer to the question, "Why do you have a record system?"

The way to meet this situation is to make records serve a definite purpose in promoting the educational work of the school. How may records and reports be used for the improvement of the work in the school? This chapter will be devoted to answering this question.

RECORD OF CONSTITUENCY

1. WHAT IS YOUR CONSTITUENCY? The Sunday School's system of records and reports should give the superintendent a clear picture of the constituency which his organization is to serve. It should also show how successfully this constituency is being

served. Every Sunday School must be responsible for the religious education *(a)* of the members of the church and their families, and *(b)* of those in the community at large who have no other church connection or preference. One measure of success must always be the effectiveness with which this constituency is reached.

2. BUILDING UP A LIST OF PROSPECTS. This suggests at once that the system of records and reports should provide for frequent comparisons between the list of members in the Sunday School and the members in the church and their families. It suggests, further, that when a new pupil is registered from a family outside the church, a careful record should be made of the other members of his family, showing their church and Sunday School connections or interests. This will provide a valuable prospective list. It suggests still further that community surveys should frequently be made, preferably in coöperation with other Church Schools, so that a prospective list covering the entire community may be made up.

3. BRINGING IN THE PROSPECTS. The alert secretary will make the comparisons between prospective lists and the actual membership graphic by means of charts and diagrams. The wide-awake superintendent will be on the alert constantly to see that plans are in process for reducing the prospective list through transfer to the active list. Particularly will

he strive to keep the prospective list from becoming larger through the addition of delinquent members from his school—but more of this later. It has been said that the superintendent should "study less in the book of Numbers and more in the book of Acts." Mere numbers do not spell success. It is true, however, that one measure of success is the ratio between the constituency of a given school and the actual attending membership.

4. WHEN IS A MEMBER A MEMBER? A word should be said about a desirable way of accepting new members. A person who signifies his intention to become a member of the school should be registered on that very day and not be required to be on probation for three weeks. It is the school which is on probation! Let it exert its utmost to hold him as a member after he has once decided to join. Who is a better prospect for becoming a permanent member than one who has once come to sample our goods?

ATTENDANCE FIGURES AND THEIR MEANING

1. NO GUIDANCE IN GROSS FIGURES. The attendance figures furnish the superintendent one of the best guides for deciding where his efforts in behalf of the improvement of the school should be placed. But merely "counting noses" is not enough. Most schools keep figures on attendance, but they mean very little because mere figures on attendance give no basis for deciding how many *ought to attend*. A

school of fifty in attendance may be doing better work than a school of five hundred. It all depends on how many pupils it has a right to expect.

2. WHAT DOES "AVERAGE ATTENDANCE" MEAN? The best index to the healthy condition of a school is the percentage of average attendance as compared with that of the anticipated attendance. A word of explanation is in order here. What do we mean by "anticipated attendance"? It is the total number of pupils who might be expected to attend on any given day. This is not quite the same as what is usually called the "enrollment," for that includes names of persons who for one reason or another cannot be expected to attend. The new International System of Records and Reports reserves the term "enrollment" for all who during any given year are connected with the school. It uses the term "attending membership" for what has been called the "anticipated attendance." According to this plan, a pupil becomes an attending member on the day he first signifies his intention of joining the school, and is removed from the attending-membership list when he is known to have permanently withdrawn or, for any reason whatever, has been absent more than three successive sessions.

The percentage of average attendance for any session is found by dividing the actual attendance (of attending members, exclusive of visitors) by the total attending membership, as defined above. The percentage of attendance for any period of sessions is the average attendance divided by the average attending membership.

3. THE VALUE OF AVERAGE ATTENDANCE FIGURES. How may these figures on percentage of attendance be of help to the superintendent in his work of supervision? He should make a careful study every week of the attendance in his school. The secretary should furnish reports which will make such study easy. When the average in any class or department, or in the school as a whole, runs high, it is a pretty sure sign that things are in a healthy condition and that the pupils are interested and satisfied. Conversely, when the percentage of attendance runs low, it is a danger sign indicating the need for a careful inspection. Perhaps the trouble is due to very bad weather or some other equally temporary cause. On the other hand, the cause may be one which requires that something be done about it at once. Perhaps a class is dissatisfied with its teacher. Perhaps the morale of a whole department has slumped. Perhaps the follow-up system has broken down. Whatever the cause may be, it should be discovered as speedily as possible and steps taken for its removal.

4. WHAT OUGHT THE AVERAGE ATTENDANCE TO BE? A normal question at this point would be, "What percentage of attendance should be considered as indicating a good condition in the school?" No general answer can be given, because no studies

have been made to determine what is possible. Public schools attain an average of 90 per cent or over. The oft-repeated statement that the average attendance of Sunday Schools is but 50 per cent of the enrollment is based on the old practice of keeping everyone on the roll indefinitely, even though it is certain that many will never again be active. If our calculations are based on attending membership as described above, this figure will be increased materially. The International Standard specifies that the average attendance should be 70 to 100 per cent and allows no credit if it is less than 70 per cent. On the basis of his own experience the author feels that the Sunday School should find it possible to maintain an average attendance of 70 to 85 per cent of the attending membership.

WHAT ABOUT LATE COMERS?

The figures on promptness of pupils and leaders are also a valuable index to the health of a school. A large number of late comers is a sure indication of a lack of serious purpose and healthy interest on the part of both pupils and leaders.

1. WHEN IS A PUPIL TARDY? The number of late comers should always be figured on the basis of the hour and minute set for the opening of the school. If the pupil comes after that time, he is late, even though the leader may commit the crime of beginning late and actually start the session *after* this pupil

arrives. Teachers should be counted tardy if they are not present at least ten minutes before the hour of opening. The practice of counting members on time if they come during the singing of the first hymn cannot be too severely denounced since it teaches slovenly habits.

2. How Many Late Comers Should We Expect? The percentage of those who are tardy is found by dividing the number of those who actually come late by the total number attending that day. Just what this figure might normally be expected to be has not been determined by careful investigation. Ideally, of course, it should be zero, but we are dealing with things as they are. The International Standard suggests 0 to 15 per cent, and allows no credit to a school if its percentage of late comers runs above 15. Any high percentage of tardiness is an indication to the superintendent that some special effort for improvement is needed.

A STUDY OF WITHDRAWALS

1. Why Do Pupils Quit? Another time when a superintendent should watch his records and reports very carefully is when pupils leave his school. The reasons for this must be discovered. No doubt some feel that the plan of removing pupils from the attending-membership list if they are absent three or more times is too drastic. Yet what better incentive can classes and departments have for an immediate

follow-up, particularly if the system provides that the reason for every removal shall be recorded? Such a plan will give the superintendent a wonderful opportunity to know where his school is failing to give satisfaction.

2. GOOD AND POOR REASONS FOR WITHDRAWAL. Withdrawals from the school, whether they be temporary or permanent, may be classified as being for either satisfactory or unsatisfactory reasons. Reasons of the former type are: removal from the community, illness, death, joining another Sunday School (under certain circumstances), temporary absence from the community. Reasons of the latter kind are such vague excuses as: "too tired," "slept too long," "went out visiting for the day." In most schools the majority of the absences are of the latter kind. They indicate a lack of keen interest on the part either of parents or of pupils. In so far as such absences occur, the school has failed to make itself of indispensable value to its pupils. Whenever there are considerable numbers of permanent withdrawals for unsatisfactory reasons, or when there are large numbers of temporary withdrawals on account of three or more absences for unsatisfactory reasons, the superintendent has his own barometer of success. If he is desirous of improving his school, he must be constantly on the alert to reduce these numbers to a minimum. He should have in operation a follow-up system which will not allow a single absence to go

by without the reason's being known. Such follow-up will work marvels in reducing the number of absences.[1]

THE PUPIL'S PERMANENT RECORD

The permanent record card of each pupil will furnish valuable data to the superintendent and his coworkers in the pursuit of their work. On this card should appear something of the pupil's life history—date of birth, baptism, Church membership, members of family, record of progress in public school, record of progress in Sunday School, and so forth. It will furnish the basis for adapting the work of the school to each individual.

The record of age and public-school progress, for example, should help in making the pupil's classification in the Sunday School. Many schools are adopting the practice of grading the pupil on the basis of his grade in public school. The writer believes that, considered from all angles, this is the most satisfactory basis for grading. It does, however, create occasional difficulties. Sometimes the work a pupil does in Sunday School is better or worse than his average performance in day school. This may be so pronounced as to require special consideration. And what of the pupil who skips a grade in public school, or fails to be promoted? In all such cases the general rule should be applied with discretion.

[1] In connection with the problem of absences the reader will find of interest a special study which has been made on this subject. See "Why Pupils Miss Sunday School," by O. W. Walters, in The International Journal of Religious Education, July, 1930.

Make exceptions where exceptions seem advisable, but only on adequate grounds. The permanent record card should help to give the data on which such decisions are based.

THE ADMINISTRATION OF RECORDS

We must conclude then, that a good system of records is essential to the educational improvement of the school. And a good secretary is essential to a good system of records. He holds one of the most important offices in the school.

A superintendent will do well to devote a liberal share of his time to the supervision of his record system. Most of the elements in it should be reduced to routine. It should provide such data as are needed for educational administration, and no data which are not needed. It should provide for such regular reports as will enable the superintendent to see the progress of his school at a glance, for each week, month, quarter, year, or any other period into which the work may be divided.

Reports consist of the orderly arrangement of the data revealed by the records, and it should be possible to take off an accurate report at any time with a minimum of effort. In addition to the regular reports to the superintendent, there should be quarterly or annual reports to the church as a whole, and to the denomination and the council of religious education as requested. The making of such reports represents no great task if the records are well kept.

Through the International Council of Religious Education a large number of denominations have coöperated in producing a system of records which is now in process of experimentation. The purpose of this system is to provide a plan for keeping records with educational value. By this system the general superintendent and every department head will know every Sunday the exact status of the department or the whole school. Every pupil is accounted for every Sunday, a regular follow-up system is provided, and, if the records are properly kept, no pupil is lost from the school without conscientious effort to retain him. The system is issued in two degrees of complexity, and beyond the minimum essentials a wide latitude is given the local church for making adaptations.

A few forms from this system are reproduced in the following pages, primarily for the purpose of illustrating how this problem of keeping satisfactory records may be solved in a simple manner.

Form 9A. DEPARTMENT OR SCHOOL RECORD

SYMBOLS
Pupil - - - - - - - - - - *P*
Officers, Teachers, and Other Leaders - *L*

Report of .... Department or School

SYMBOLS
Enrolment - - - - - - *E*
Additions by transfer - - =
Loss by transfer - - - - O

Withdrawn temporarily - *WT*
Return - - - - - - - - - - *R*
Withdrawn permanently - *W*

Date ....

Class, Grade, Dept., Other Group	Attending Membership at Preceding Session		Admitted			Withdrawn				Attending Membership This Session		Inactive in Attendance		Present		Absent		Visitors	Offering
			Pupils	Leaders		Pupils		Leaders											
	P	L	E=	R	E=R	W	O	WT	W	O	WT	P	L	P	L	P	L	P	L	P	L		

Totals	
Last (week, quarter, year)	

Remarks:

34194

International System of Church School Records and Reports
Copyright, 1929. International Council of Religious Education. Printed in U. S. A.
5 South Wabash Avenue, Chicago, Ill.

Records and Reports

Form 2B. REGISTRATION AND PERMANENT RECORD BLANK
(Boys and Men)

Date................................

Name in full.. Phone..............................

Address..

*Age on last birthday............ *Born: Month............... Day............... Year............... Baptized?...............

Name of public school or college.. Grade or college year........................

If not in school, nature and address of business...

Church school last attended...

Member of what church (name and location)...

*Father's (or guardian's) name..

*Church he attends...

*Mother's (or guardian's) name...

*Church she attends...

Entered: Department............... Grade............ Class or Other Group..

Teacher or Leader..

Assigned by..

Registration date..

*Need not be filled in for adults.   (over)

(Reverse Side)

Record of Progress in This School

(For additional items)

School Year	Public School Grade	Church School Department, Grade, Class, Other Group	Program or Curriculum	Teacher or Leader		

Withdrawal: Date.................... Reason...

34551

Actual size of card 6x4 inches

Improving Your Sunday School

Form 1B-1A. RELIGIOUS CENSUS BLANK.

Family Name (last name only) .... Nationality.................................... Race...............

Address .... Apartment No...................; Phone...............

Given Name	Age under 24	Occupation or Public School Grade	Church Relationship (Give name of church; check relationship)				Church School Relationship (Give name of school; check relationship)		
			Name of Church	Member	Attends	Prefers	Name of School	Attends	Pre
Father									
Mother									
Children at home									
Others[1] in family									
Detached Individual[2]									

Further information: (Children out of town at school or out of town at work, etc.)

Reported by ....

Date ....

[1] Give the full name and indicate under "Remarks" whether a certain relative, servant, roomer, etc., is listed.
[2] A person living apart from any local family or household connections.

International System of Church School Records and Reports
Copyright, 1929. International Council of Religious Education. Printed in U. S. A.
5 South Wabash Avenue, Chicago, Ill.

Actual size of card 8x5 inches

Chapter VIII

THE USE OF STANDARDS AND GOALS

SHOCKED BUT HAPPY! The Eighth Street Sunday School was once cited in the national convention as one of the best in the entire denomination. Ten years had passed yet the tradition still lingered. The workers thought of their school as one which was perfect beyond all possibility of improvement. In the meantime the march of progress in religious education had passed them by and left them hopelessly behind the times.

It happened that about this time the city council of religious education was encouraging the use of the new International Church School Standard. Eighth Street School was one of the first to be studied by this Standard. As the group of workers met for the scoring, they were at first smugly complacent, then surprised, then good-naturedly discomfited. In the face of the searching questions asked in the Standard, they found that they could conscientiously rate themselves as only a 50 per cent school! In that hour they realized the folly of resting on the laurels of bygone days. In that hour they stood convicted as back numbers. But in that hour, too, they caught a vision of what might be done to make their school a better school. A comprehensive plan was adopted for the improvement of the school, the results of which will probably go on for years to come. Eighth Street Sunday School is living in the past no longer!

A Friend in Need. John Layton was frankly discouraged. For one year he had been superintendent of the Greenbrier Sunday School, and it seemed to him that his efforts had resulted in failure. He had come into the community a few years before, after years of experience in a well-organized, graded Sunday School, and had been shocked by the conditions he found in the Greenbrier School. He was zealous for a better school, not only because he felt that the community needed it, but also because his own children must receive their religious training in that school. When, therefore, they had asked him to become superintendent he had willingly accepted the invitation, with high hopes of what might be accomplished. The year had gone by, but the expected results had not been forthcoming.

It was not that the workers had not treated Mr. Layton with respect and honor. They had been more than kind. The trouble seemed to be that his high ideals came to naught because the workers took him for granted and paid little heed to his appeals for improvement. The school moved on at a dead level of half interest and half enthusiasm with results which were far below what they should have been.

At this point Mr. Layton decided to make a study of the school by means of the Church School Standard. He discovered this interesting fact: While the Standard upheld an ideal which was little beyond that which he had advocated throughout the year, coming as it did with official indorsement and authority, it commanded a respect which his words had failed to win. In other words, the Standard put into his hands an instrument with which he could attain some of the ideals which he had always held for his school. Self-evaluation on the items of the Standard soon convicted this group of workers of educational sin, and led to the inevitable question, "What must we do to be saved?" From this point forward Mr. Layton found the road toward improvement of his school very much easier.

LET THE STANDARD SAY IT! Every superintendent is faced constantly with the problem of the improvement of the individual workers. Here is a department principal who has not caught the true meaning of worship. There is a teacher who is too self-satisfied, who ought to be shown a higher ideal. To approach these workers directly will often result in heartache and bad feeling because Sunday School workers have not yet learned the meaning of supervision.

In a certain Sunday School the superintendent solved this problem of personal improvement through the use of the Standard. By putting into the hands of the workers copies of the Standard and asking them to rate themselves carefully on points which he

indicated for them, he made impersonal the suggestions which might otherwise have caused resentment.
This study of the Standard now and again opened
the way for personal conferences. These conferences
were pervaded by a desire on the part of both the
superintendent and the teacher to work together in
finding the way to the attainment of the ideal. This
is a very different matter from the superintendent's
setting an arbitrary goal which the teacher is asked
to attain.

HELPING THEM TO HELP THEMSELVES. The
workers in Bethel Sunday School had conscientiously
tried to make theirs the best school it could possibly
become. They had worked as a unit on this common
enterprise, each contributing what he could and learning from what others were contributing. They had
carried their work as far as they could without outside assistance. What they needed most was to see
their situation objectively from the outside, without
the prides and prejudices which make people blind to
the defects of their own work.

The Church School Standard furnished the means
for this objective evaluation. Here was an impartial
judge who would help them to see themselves as others
saw them. A diligent study of the requirements of
the Standard and a careful rating of their school
by its scoring directions enabled them to see the
places at which their work most needed improvement.
Thus a new impetus was given to their work, and

Bethel school was saved from that mediocrity which so easily leads into self-satisfied complacency.

WHAT IS A STANDARD?

A standard is the statement of an ideal which serves as a measuring stick for the work which is actually being done. Just as we have measures of length by means of which we may calculate distance, measures of weight by which we may calculate how heavy different objects are, so we should have a standard for Sunday Schools by means of which we may calculate the achievement of a school. When we consider the importance of checking up on ourselves to determine whether we are making progress, no matter what the work is in which we are engaged, we realize the importance of having a standard for the Sunday School.

Unfortunately our standards for measuring the work of Sunday Schools are at best very imperfect. The only real test of the work of a Sunday School is whether its pupils are learning to live the Christian life. There is, however, no way of testing progress in Christian living except life itself. If we should wait until all the pupils in our Sunday School have lived their lives, and then make a careful study of each of them, we should have a fairly accurate measure of the effectiveness of the work we are now doing. But that would be too late to influence our work now, and now is the time that we want it to be the best it can possibly be made. We must therefore resort to some other method of measurement.

The principle on which most standards are based is that of recognition of certain conditions as essential to good religious teaching. These conditions are set down as bases on which measurement may be made. We are fairly certain that growth in Christian living demands a Christian atmosphere and purpose in the Sunday School, Christian teachers who know how to teach, opportunities for worship and service, and so forth. Hence we may put down these and other items like them as the bases for our standard. To be sure, a perfect score on all such items does not always insure Christian growth on the part of all the pupils who attend the school. Let us bear this in mind and avoid insisting on a mechanical perfection; let us lean constantly toward the spiritual outcomes which are the goals of all our efforts.

Some avoid the use of the term "standard" in designating such instruments as we have here described, and speak of them rather as "programs of work" or "goals." However, the word "standard" is in common use, and we need not hesitate to employ it so long as we understand what we mean thereby.

Within the past five years the International Council of Religious Education has carried through an extensive piece of work in the building of standards in religious education. These have now been published under the general name, "International Standards in Religious Education." The system includes two Standards for the Sunday Church School, one simple (B) and one more complex (A); a Standard for the Vacation Church School; a Standard for the Week Day Church School; and Standards for each of the departments of the Church School.

These International Standards have been officially adopted by a number of the denominations coöperating through the International Council. Some denominations, on the other hand, have developed their own standards, as in the case of the "Programs of Work" of the Methodist Episcopal Church, South. The discussion in this chapter is based on the International Standards, though in most cases it applies equally well to all good standards.

THE USE OF STANDARDS

The illustrations given earlier in this chapter will serve to show a few of the many ways in which standards may be used for the improvement of religious education in the church. These uses of a standard may be summarized as:

1. GUIDANCE. By indicating the important things to stress, and the quality of attainment to be sought, standards serve as a guide to the building of a good school. In this capacity a standard may be used much as an architect's blue print is used in constructing a house. A careful study of the Inter-

national Standards, for instance, cannot but result in improved work, irrespective of any effort to rate the school.

2. MEASUREMENT. Through a plan of scoring it is possible to evaluate the work which is being done in the Sunday School. This is an important help to guidance, for it is through measurement that present attainments may be determined. To use an everyday expression, it is the measurement phase of a standard which "puts teeth into" guidance.

Above all things, superintendents should bear in mind that a standard is a tool by which better work may be accomplished. It is not a master, but a slave. Striving for the attainment of the points of the standard, simply because it is the standard, should be zealously avoided. Superintendents should let the standard serve as a means for recognizing that which is most important in their work, and use it with that freedom which should characterize all the work of the true leader.

AS A SUPERVISORY DEVICE

Consistent with the purpose of this book, our purpose in the above discussion has been to answer the question, How may standards best be used in supervision, that is, in the improvement of teaching? They should prove a great help to the superintendent in the more intimate work of improving the individual members in his staff of officers and teachers.

The Use of Standards and Goals

The superintendent should look upon the Sunday School standard as a tool which will help him to do his work better. A careful study of the standard will be the very best way for him to see the whole task of his school in its proper relationship. In the same way it will help him to show his workers what the goals are toward which he is endeavoring to guide the school. A comprehensive plan of administration of standards would include the following items:

1. STUDY. There should be a careful study of the pamphlet itself, so that its various items may be fully understood. All teachers and officers should share in this study, which will make excellent programs for a series of workers' conferences. The study should be made in the light of the conditions in the local school, with the question constantly raised: What does this mean in our school? Through such study many workers will get a new vision of their tasks.

2. SCORING. After the standard is thoroughly understood, it should be used in scoring the school. It is best to appoint one individual or a small committee to be responsible for the scoring. Whenever possible, however, the entire group of workers should be used in gathering data. Some of the facts may be secured right in the workers' conference meeting; others will need to be secured when the school is in session; still others will require investigation outside of the Sunday School hour. Sometimes it may be

stimulating to have the workers share in deciding the scores in the light of the facts available, even though this may not assure so accurate a score as if the scoring were done by a small committee. The scores should be recorded in permanent form for future reference.

3. REPORTING. The results of the scoring should be reported to the entire group of workers. A wall chart will be of help in doing this. Plenty of opportunity should be given for discussion of the scores assigned to the various items of the standard. Ways and means through which the school may be improved so as to make a higher score should also be freely discussed. Several meetings of the workers' conference may well be devoted to this report and discussion. Out of this study should grow a program for the improvement of the school.

4. IMPROVEMENT. A definite period should be set aside during which the improvements which have been agreed upon may be made. This may occupy a quarter, two quarters, or a year. It is well to plan to do one or a few things at a time in order not to confuse the workers. Each one should understand clearly what he is expected to do in order to effect the desired improvement in the school.

At the end of this period of improvement the time is ripe for a new measurement of the school and another period of improvement. Care should be taken that all new workers who may have joined the staff from time to time are brought fully into the process so that they, too, may be benefited by the standard.

While during such a program of study and improvement efforts are directed toward the work in the school, the teachers themselves will grow more competent through this experience. This is the most important outcome to be desired, even though it comes as a by-product. This is sufficient argument for allowing the workers to share as fully as possible in the work of study and measurement.

Chapter IX

IMPROVING THE WORKING CONDITIONS

In discussing ways in which teaching in the Sunday School may be improved, much stress has been laid upon the improvement of the worker. This is putting emphasis in the right place. In addition to this, however, must be emphasized the necessity of providing the worker with a suitable place in which to work. The building in which the Sunday School meets constitutes the teacher's workshop. The equipment which is put into that building constitutes the tools with which he works. A good workman must have the very best instruments with which to do his work.

THE REAL AND THE IDEAL

Most of us like to dream about what the result would be if we could erect a Sunday School building just as we think it should be built, and then equip it in accordance with our most cherished ideal. Comparatively few superintendents, however, are privileged to build the place in which the Sunday School meets. Most of them have inherited a building and a certain type of equipment with which they must work.

Why then should time be spent in discussing ideal conditions? What use can there be in talking about what ought to be when in the nature of the case we must work with what is? Will not such discussion serve to discourage rather than to help? There are two answers to be made to these questions.

1. IDEALIZE THE REAL! In order to improve what is, the superintendent must have a clear picture of what ought to be. There is nothing so deadening as entire satisfaction with things as they are. A constant vision of what ought to be is a very necessary step in the direction of improvement.

Having once attained such a vision the superintendent is in a position to study things as they are. He will then be able to see what there is in the present equipment which is satisfactory and what needs to be changed. He will be able to consider what changes can most readily be made. Step by step, a little here and a little there, the ideal will begin to emerge out of the real. While many buildings cannot be made into modern educational plants any more than old log cabins can be made into palatial residences, most buildings in use at the present time can be greatly improved if the ideal is kept in mind.

2. REALIZE THE IDEAL! Church buildings come and go, but Sunday Schools go on forever. In place of the old buildings of to-day there will some day be new buildings which will be adequate, if proper thought has been given as to what ideal conditions require. Sunday School workers must do what so many families are doing: they must look far into the future to that home which is eventually to be built.

They must study Church School architecture and the requirements for good educational buildings. They must dream about plans, and agitate for that ideal which the future will some day make real. This is the surest way to be ready for the day when the building of a new plant becomes an actual project.

SOME BASIC PRINCIPLES

From this point forward we shall have in mind largely those things which can be done by a superintendent to improve the building and equipment which he now has. Certain basic principles should be borne in mind when the improvements which may be made are considered.

1. EQUIPMENT MUST BE BASED ON NEEDS. The first question which a superintendent should ask is, What is the program which this school should carry out? The second question will logically follow: What do we need in the way of rooms and equipment to carry out this program?

This suggests that a careful survey must be made to determine needs. For how many pupils must this school prepare, not merely for this year, but for ten, twenty, or thirty years to come? What kind of activities are to be carried on? These and many other questions must be asked and answered before a Building Committee may begin to draw up plans.

2. THE BUILDING AND EQUIPMENT MUST BE ADEQUATE FOR THE ACTIVITIES TO BE CARRIED ON.

This principle is so self-evident that it would not be necessary to state it, were it not for the fact that all too often it is not observed. When a Building Committee which knows nothing about a modern program of religious education presumes to plan a Church School plant it is time to call a halt. A few dollars spent in securing the advice of an expert will often mean many dollars saved in costly alterations after the building is erected.

This question of the activities to be carried on is very difficult, even for experts in religious education. It is difficult because no one quite dares to predict what developments will take place in the course of the next fifty years. Some buildings which were considered modern ten years ago are becoming obsolete because of changes in the administration of religious education. Certain basic activities, however, will need to be provided for, such as worship, teaching, dramatics, play and recreation, socials.

3. Equipment Must Be in Harmony with the Best Trends in Education. This principle requires constant alertness to the development of educational science. One educational principle which is quite definitely established is that of gradation. Schools must provide for separation into groups so that each pupil may work with those of approximately his own age and participate in a program of religious education adapted to that age. Demands must, of course, be flexible. Some schools can grade more

closely than others. Even the smallest Sunday
School should, however, seek to have the younger
children separated from the rest of the school for
worship, and to have classes with an age range which
does not go beyond that of the usual departmental
group. If it is at all possible, there should be at
least one class for each grade of each department.
Proper grading by ages is of more importance than
the separation of boys from girls. The building
should provide some privacy for the separate groups.
In many cases this requires some ingenious work on
the part of the superintendent either to provide for
separation in a one-room building which now exists
or to arrange for such remodeling of the building as
will care for the graded school.

The prevailing plan for the separation of groups
has been to provide an assembly room for each
department, and, wherever possible, classrooms for
the small classes into which the department is divided
after the assembly period. Thus it is necessary to
provide for two meeting places for each pupil. Some
of the more recent tendencies may have a decided
influence on this plan.

a. In order to provide a worship assembly room
more suitable than the departmental room, some
churches have built a separate worship chapel, beautifully arranged and used only for the worship period.
By bringing in different departments at different
times, this room serves two or more departments on

a given Sunday. For older departments the church auditorium may be used for worship.

b. Some schools, instead of dividing the school into departments and having a departmental assembly followed by grouping into small classes, have divided the school on the basis of grades. An entire school grade is assigned to a given teacher and a number of assistants. This grade has what is spoken of as an "integrated program," that is, the teacher provides for worship, instruction, service activity, and so forth, as each may fit into the work of a particular Sunday. In other words, the one leader has the entire Sunday School hour. It is not our purpose here to discuss either the merits or demerits of this plan, but simply to recognize it as a trend which must be borne in mind in planning for a Church School plant and its equipment.

c. A third development of which account must be taken is our changing method of teaching. We no longer have pupils seated in rigid rows for instruction, with the teacher doing all the work. Provision is now made for much free activity. Our curriculum is based on doing rather than on hearing. This requires larger classrooms, a more flexible type of equipment, and working materials which were not considered necessary under the older plans.

4. The Church School Building and Equipment Should Have Beauty. The International Standards require that the quality and appearance

of Sunday School rooms shall be at least up to the prevailing standards of the homes in the community. The Sunday School should be a place to which a pupil may go with joy. It should be a place in which he is comfortable, and from which he may carry memories which are pleasant. There is scarcely a Sunday School in this land which cannot make some improvement in this respect. Some of the most unsightly rooms which the author has ever seen have been rooms in which classes of boys and girls met for instruction in religion.

5. THE CHURCH SCHOOL BUILDING AND EQUIPMENT SHOULD TAKE ACCOUNT OF THE PRINCIPLE OF ECONOMY. Due to the fact that the Sunday School meets for so brief a time each week, the total cost per pupil per teaching hour is very high. Saving should be effected wherever possible, as long as it is consistent with the best educational work. Some schools, for instance, use the same rooms twice on the same Sunday by having different groups meet at different hours. Others are giving thought primarily to utility with attractiveness, and secondarily to such further appointments as may be desirable but are very costly.

6. THE BUILDING AND EQUIPMENT MUST PROVIDE FOR QUALITY AND PERMANENCE. So many Sunday Schools buy their equipment as though they expected to operate for only a year or two. They fail to take account of the fact that in all cases it is best to buy

good materials. Makers of cheap folding chairs have prospered at the expense of the children who have used the chairs. It is far better to make progress slowly by securing good equipment than to buy cheap materials which become warped, broken and unsightly a short time after they have been installed.

TYPES OF EQUIPMENT

It is impossible to name all the items of equipment which a Sunday School should have, because their number will depend upon the educational program which is being developed. It is possible, however, to suggest a few of the things which should be included. Following Johnny as he comes to Sunday School on a particular Sunday will show what is needed.

1. As Johnny comes into the building where does he go first? There should be a place where he may hang his coat and hat. He should not be required to keep them on his chair where they will be in his way throughout the session, or to keep them on and be uncomfortable. This applies to teachers as well as to pupils. Some kind of coat rack should be provided for every member of the school.

2. Next Johnny will probably go to a worship assembly room. We have already indicated that this room should be made as worshipful as possible. If it can be modeled after the plan of a worship chapel, so much the better. In this room he should find a

comfortable seat—a pew if possible, or some good chapel seat—fitted to his size so that his feet may be placed comfortably on the floor. It should be dignified and conducive to rest and quiet.

3. Convenient to his hand he should find a hymn book, that is, if he is old enough to use a hymn book. This hymn book should be in good condition, a worthy vehicle for the hymns he is to sing. It should contain the very best hymns for religious education which the English language provides. In the room there should be a musical instrument properly tuned; there should be an altar or a table from which the leader of worship may minister; there should be offering plates which may be utilized in the service of giving.

4. After a service of worship Johnny will proceed to a class session. What are some of the things which he should find in his classroom?

a. He should find a chair for his use which is suited to his height, comfortable, and possessed of at least some beauty. In addition to the chair he should have some working space, a table or a desk. The prevailing practice has been to conduct small classes around tables, but this is by no means the most practical way of handling a class. Unless the class is very small the pupils are crowded; some of them cannot see the teacher very well; they are in each other's way; and, if any one of them is inclined to have a streak of mischief, the temptation to do something naughty under the cover of the table is very great. Some schools have replaced the chairs and tables with tablet armchairs, or, better still, chair desks. These are movable pieces of furniture which may readily be shifted as the activity of the class requires. They enable the teacher to place the pupils in such a position as to assure the best harmony and industry for the group.

b. There should be a place where Johnny may keep his things, that is, the things which he does not carry home with him. A cabinet or other type of storage space should provide a place of his own.

c. There should be books in the room, textbooks and reference books. These books may be brought from the Sunday School library each Sunday, or they may belong to the teacher, or they may have been secured for this particular class. Also attractive bookcases will add materially to the appearance of the classroom.

d. In the classroom there should be a blackboard, so placed that it may be used by both teacher and pupils. With this blackboard there

A COMBINATION BULLETIN BLACKBOARD

may be combined a bulletin board on which notices, pictures, or exhibits of handwork are displayed.

9

e. The walls of the room should display some attractive pictures. These pictures should be interpreted to Johnny and his classmates, and should form a part of the atmosphere which they imbibe Sunday after Sunday.

f. If the class is large, and if the teacher intends to carry on some worship activity in addition to the usual teaching work, the room should also have a piano.

5. In the course of the week Johnny may come to the church for activities of various sorts under the auspices of the Sunday School. He may come to play basketball, or he may come to participate in dramatics. Whatever these outside activities may be, the school must provide equipment for them, such as basketballs and other athletic equipment, a stage for dramatics, costumes for dramatic activity, a kitchen where refreshments may be prepared for socials, and so forth.

6. A very important item of equipment for every Sunday School is a place where things may be stored. If the school possesses athletic equipment this must be properly kept under lock and key when it is not in use. If it has dramatic activities, there must be a place for storage of costumes. If it uses temporary scenery from time to time, there must be a place where this may be kept when not in use. Too many schools are hampered by having their rooms and halls made unsightly because they are used for storage

rooms. No church should be built without ample room in which to store things which are not regularly in use.

PRACTICAL PLANS

In conclusion we shall describe a few plans which may help to start the superintendent in his program for the improvement of his Church School building and equipment:

1. Perhaps the first step to be taken is that of "selling" the idea to his constituency. There are various ways in which this may be approached. One school accomplished it by arranging for its workers an excursion to a church which was well equipped in order that they might get a new ideal of what could be done. As they examined the equipment in this church, they exclaimed again and again, "Why, we could do that!" The result was an attitude of desiring improvement and a willingness to support proposals for various improvements as they were made. Another church planned a parent-teacher dinner at which the work of the school was discussed. The needs of the school for better equipment were laid before the parents and the suggestion was made that perhaps they would like to start a fund for improving the equipment of the Sunday School. The suggestion met with a ready response. A Primary Department solved this problem by having a Parents' Sunday in order that fathers and mothers might see the work of the department. It was readily appar-

ent to these parents that the workers were handicapped by lack of equipment. Out of this grew the suggestion that each parent pay the price of a chair for his child.

2. Perhaps the best way to assure regular improvement in the equipment of the school is to provide an item in the budget through which the most necessary improvements may be made year by year. If this is done the board of religious education will be forced to face again and again the question, "What shall we do next?" It should also be said in this connection that when a new building is to be erected, the cost of equipment for the Church School should be included as a part of the initial cost. It is pathetic to see how beautifully some of our better churches have furnished the church auditorium, the ladies' parlor, and the kitchen, and how barren they have left the Sunday School rooms. The thought seems to be that the Sunday School may gradually equip itself. This is a wrong approach. A few hundred dollars added to the initial cost of the building looks small. When, however, that amount is added to the expenses of a year, which include interest on a heavy building debt, it looms so large that there is great difficulty in getting it approved.

3. The question of providing adequate department rooms and classrooms presents a serious problem because of our changing educational practice, and also because sizes of classes and departments change

from year to year. One church solved this problem by means of temporary partitions. Modern offices are built on this plan so that the space may be divided to suit the particular needs of the organization. By means of such temporary partitions the space in a large room may readily be redistributed at small expense. If such temporary partitions are properly installed, they cannot be distinguished from actual walls.

4. The superintendent should make a constant study of the possible rearrangement of rooms so as to use them to better advantage. Often great improvement in the work of the school can be made by a better use of the space available. This may be accomplished by a simple shifting of pupils and classes in a given room, by reassigning the available rooms so as better to fit the needs of the pupils to be served (no class or department should have a permanent claim to a room), or by a judicious use of curtains or screens.

Here is an illustration:

A superintendent had long been bothered by the situation presented in his Primary Department. All the work had to be done in one room. There were ten classes. Several of the teachers were very competent, but there was always a shortage of teachers. He made a careful study of the whole situation in its relation to the work of the entire school. In consultation with the Primary principal, the following plan was worked out: An adjacent classroom was secured by shifting a Young People's class to another room. Two of the three third-grade classes were combined into one, with a membership of twelve pupils. This new class was given the best available Primary teacher, and assigned to the separate classroom. In the main room the piano was shifted to a different position so as to screen off an alcove at one end of the assembly room. This alcove was further divided by means of a screen so as to provide separation for two classes. This one supervisory effort resulted in relieving the congestion in the Primary room by removing twelve pupils and two classes, in giving the new group an excellent teacher and a separate classroom, in eliminating one teacher, and in providing two other classes with fairly satisfactory classrooms.

5. Good educational work requires the use of blackboards, and yet there are some teachers who do not

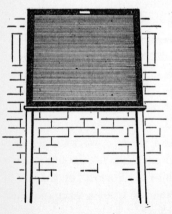

This blackboard is 3½' by 4½' and can be purchased for about five dollars. The legs are 1″ by 2″ strips screwed to the back of the frame and stained to match the woodwork. The board can be placed against the wall or other convenient backing. It is light and easily carried. It can be moved from room to room as teachers may have need for it. A dozen of these blackboards can be stored in a very small space when it is desirable to have a room cleared.

care to use blackboards. While it is desirable to have a permanent blackboard in each room, this is often not practicable. The solution is to provide a number of movable blackboards and allocate them to those teachers who most desire to use them. A very simple type of movable blackboard is shown in the accompanying illustration.

6. Much has been said in recent years about the use of curtains and screens to provide separation for classes and departments. It should be admitted that while such separation is but a makeshift it is better than nothing. If curtains and screens are used, care should be taken that they are attractive. The educational advantages gained by separation through the use of such makeshifts may be more than lost if they mar the beauty of the rooms in which they are used.

The illustration on page 136 shows a very practical screen which is both beautiful and useful. The panels are made of celotex wall board, which is a good sound deadener. The center panel is a blackboard, and for this purpose the best commercial blackboard was secured. Hence the screen provides the essential separation for two classes or departments and at the same time gives each a permanent blackboard.

7. A progressive school needs a working library. Some schools have asked each teacher to purchase a good book and donate it to the library for the use of all. These books are selected from a prepared list.

If this is done each year a gradually growing library will be provided. Magazines may also be furnished on an exchange basis.

A PRACTICAL AND INEXPENSIVE SCREEN
The panels are of wall board, with a Hyloplate blackboard in center

These are but a few suggestions of ways in which the problem of improving equipment may be handled. The alert superintendent will be studying his problem continuously, and will have his plans for improvement made perhaps years in advance of the actual carrying out of such plans.

Chapter X

SPECIAL DAYS AND SEASONS

Everybody observes special days. Families have birthdays and anniversaries to celebrate; schools have national holidays; churches have sacred festivals and seasons. But what makes special days special? Is it not that a particular individual or group attaches a peculiar significance to that particular landmark in the calendar? It follows, then, that educationally it may be just as important to make our pupils aware that certain days are special as it is to observe certain special days.

WHY SPECIAL DAYS?

Why should a Sunday School which is already crowded to the limit bother about observing special days? Not because it makes the school more interesting to the pupils. Not because special day programs are entertaining (particularly to adult visitors). Not because the announcement of a special program may draw a larger attendance. All these things, and more, may result from the observance of special days, but they must always remain in the position of by-products. The only adequate reason for observing special days is this: that the religious education of the pupils may be advanced.

Present-day trends in religious education serve to

emphasize the value of the observance of special days. We make much of teaching by means of life situations. A special day, such as Christmas or Easter, presents a very real and interesting life situation to the child. We speak of guidance and enrichment of experience as being the goal of teaching. What is more important than that we interpret the true significance of such holidays to our pupils and thus enrich their meaning? We emphasize the importance of "concomitant" learnings, that is, things learned as by-products outside the deliberate intention of the teacher. The very atmosphere which pervades the church on our great festal days is charged with suggestion which cannot help leaving its imprint on immature lives.

THE SUPERVISION OF SPECIAL DAYS

Having seen special days and seasons as opportunities for teaching religion, we are now in a position to see the relation of supervision to them. If the purpose of supervision be the improvement of teaching, then in his capacity as supervisor the superintendent must lead his workers into the fullest possible realization of the educational value of special days. He must seek to give his coworkers a true conception of what may be accomplished educationally through special days. As administrator he may take executive responsibility for the carrying out of special observances, but his success as a supervisor can be measured only by the extent to which all his workers have caught the religious value of the special days to be observed, and developed an effective method for realizing these values in their teaching work.

The fundamental principle has been laid down that the observance of special days must be an educational venture. There are six rules which may be given to superintendents for bringing this about:

1. Begin your preparations early. To use a special day educationally requires much more time than merely to prepare a special program. The time to begin intensive preparations for Christmas is immediately after Rally Day. The time to begin preparation for Easter is immediately after Christmas. This emphasis on early preparation suggests at once that the proper observance of a few special days is worth more than passing attention to the whole calendar of special days. It is possible, of course, to give very dignified attention to some days in the general program of a school or department without intensive preparation, but we are speaking here of the kind of observance which has educational value.

2. Lay primary emphasis upon the education of your leaders. Unless the department leaders and teachers have caught the spirit of the special day observance there is little chance of success. In order to get the full benefit of the indirect educational value of such a special observance the whole atmosphere of the school must be pervaded by its spirit. This can

come to pass only when there are many ready minds, sympathetic hearts, and skillful hands to help to make it so. The teachers in a Sunday School, if they come in the proper spirit, will always learn more than the pupils. Here is the supervisor's opportunity to make special days minister to the personal enrichment of his workers!

3. Center the attention of your workers on educational values. This follows as a matter of course if we are to make the observance of special days educational. You will find that workers are by no means agreed as to the true meaning of most special days, including Christmas, in the field of religious education. Let one outstanding objective be selected as a desired outcome, and then let each department group and class plan its work so that this objective may be realized.

4. Let the preparation for a special day carry part of its educational value. If it be your plan to observe Easter with an appropriate play, let it be to the participants more than a humdrum of rehearsals for one brief hour of presentation. Let it rather be an enterprise in gaining an understanding and appreciation of the characters represented as well as of the play as a whole. Let the presentation be an effort to represent to others the value which the players have already apprehended. If the observance of Christmas is to include an opportunity for everybody to give, let this be not merely blind giving but giving

as the result of an understanding of the cause, so that the gift may be made in the spirit of Him whom we remember in the observance. If Armistice Day is to be used as an occasion for peace education, let those who participate do so with understanding and sympathy because the observance of the day has been preceded by a careful study of the factors involved in settling the problems of world peace and friendship.

5. Make the primary purpose of the presentation educational. Here is where the greatest obstacle will be met by those who plan for educational results from special days—especially in connection with Christmas. People have become so accustomed to being entertained that few superintendents will have the courage to deny them that almost inalienable right. In the main, it is those who do not attend the Sunday School who dominate our festival observances. They like an "old-fashioned" Christmas. Therefore, there must be an old-fashioned Christmas observance. And so the little folks must be asked to sing and speak "pieces," not because anyone wishes to listen to their messages, but because they are so "cute."

We are maintaining that educational values must predominate in our observance of special days—for those who are the audience as well as for those who participate in the program. We mean by this that the special day must bring them something by way of enrichment for their religious lives—some new insight, some desirable emotional stirring, some sublime moment of inspiration or worship. This need not make the special day program less entertaining. The greater the pleasure, the more effective the educational value will be, other things being equal. But the pleasure must come from satisfaction of the higher impulses rather than from a mere pleasant passing away of time. Our emphasis in the observance of special days is on educational values first, with just as much of interest and entertainment as is consistent with this ideal.

6. Have a care that the by-products are also educationally desirable. How often have children and their parents gone away from services planned to commemorate the coming of good will among men with anything but good will in their hearts because some other child received greater honor! How often has the church witnessed a mad scramble to receive, in the face of its teaching that "it is more blessed to give than to receive"!

Occasionally a child comes to our door with a plaintive appeal: "Won't you please buy a ticket? It's for the church!" Never a word of what value I am to receive for my money! Never a thought that I am to consider anything but the possibility of paying over some money "for the church," whether I can attend the program covered by the ticket or not! What must be the by-products in the lives of these little agents resulting from the activities of a church which sees in special observances only an opportunity to make money and is willing to exploit its children in so doing!

A FEW TYPICAL DAYS

It may be well to point out the educational value of a few of the special days and seasons commonly observed, and make some suggestions toward their proper observance. All special occasions cannot be treated—the canon is not closed, and our space is limited. A few must serve as typical.

1. RALLY DAY. This presents an opportunity not so much for recovering from summer losses, or for reopening the school in case it has been closed for the summer, as for leading the members to dedicate themselves to a new period of service. Too much has been made of the mass attendance idea for Rally Day. Let it serve, rather, as an occasion for educating young and old in the meaning of religious education, for leading them to see their need of what it has to offer, and for emphasizing the responsibility which each must bear for his own religious growth.

2. RELIGIOUS EDUCATION WEEK. As these pages are being prepared, the International Council of Religious Education is adopting a plan for a Religious Education Week, to be tried out in churches and communities in the fall of 1930. The purpose of the week is to help religious education to come into its own in both the church and the community. Every church or group of churches will be free to make such

use of this week as best fits the local situation. The week will open with Rally Day and close with the service of promotion and the installation of workers for the new year.

The program for Religious Education Week should provide for a varied approach to the church, and, through interchurch coöperation, to the community. It should provide for a rallying of the forces. It should give an opportunity for placing religious education before the entire church. It should bring together parents and church officials with teachers and officers for the study of the religious and moral welfare of the child. It should make an impact on the community through the press, through the use of posters, and through community surveys. It should provide for family fellowship within the church. The interesting possibilities for such a week are almost unlimited.

3. HARVEST HOME. This presents an opportunity to emphasize in a special way the providence of God. It offers an opportunity to fill common things with religious significance. But the approach should be concrete and not abstract. In a Beginners Department one Sunday the leader, wishing to take advantage of the Harvest Home festival in the church, attempted to interpret "harvest" to the children. "Does anyone here know the meaning of harvest?" she inquired. Of course no one did. "I know it is a very unusual word," added the leader, and proceeded

with an abstract definition. There is more truth than charity in saying that this leader completely failed in achieving the objective for this session. Yet there were two ways in which the session could have been conducted so as to register very vividly in the lives of the children: (*a*) The leader might have brought into the room a display of fruit, vegetables, and grain (a very real addition by way of decoration to the barren room) and centered the program around the thought of thankfulness for the harvest, or (*b*) she might have taken the children into the church auditorium, which had been beautifully decorated with the products of the harvest, conducting the worship service there and centering it around the interpretation of the meaning of these decorations in the church. Incidentally, this would have afforded an opportunity for introducing the pastor into the service, and making the church more real in the lives of the children.

4. THANKSGIVING. The close proximity of this holiday to Christmas makes it difficult to give it the attention it deserves. Perhaps this is not a serious drawback in view of the fact that public schools are giving a great deal of attention to it. The life-situation approach does not imply that we are simply to let the pupils do what they have already done in public school. Unless religious education can add a distinctive value to any day, we had better not take the time for observing it.

When Thanksgiving is specially observed, effort should be made to center attention on the idea of thanksgiving and of rendering to God what belongs to him. If we can but in a measure counteract the pagan gluttony which has become characteristic of this day, and give the day a spiritual meaning, the effort will have been worth while.

5. CHRISTMAS. No detail on the observance of this season need here be given. The season should extend over a number of weeks. The outstanding message should be good will among men. This permits of the joys of both giving and receiving, but at no time should the receiving attitude overshadow the spreading of good will through giving. So much that is pagan has sprung up around this season that the Sunday School will do well to hold fast to the distinctive Christian meaning of the day and make that meaning a vital experience to its pupils.

6. EASTER. This season has usually been made an occasion for personal dedication to the Master and his cause. This is right, provided we safeguard two points: (a) Teachers should avoid giving the impression that such dedication once a year is enough, and that the rest of the year may be lived without this need for close fellowship with the Master; (b) They must avoid making the appeal so abstract as to be devoid of all tangible results outside of an emotional upheaval. Dedication should have some definite setting in personal life and conduct. The call to life

service may well be made the keynote of our work throughout the weeks preceding Easter.

7. MISSIONARY DAY. This is a vital part of the Church School program. It saves the pupil from a self-centered and parochial conception of religion and enables him to see his Christian responsibility for the elements in his own community who need Christ. On the basis of this definite relationship with human needs, and the Great Commission of Jesus, "Go ye into all the world, and preach the gospel to the whole creation," there can be developed in the pupil an attitude of Christian responsibility for classes and races in his own country and in the world, that men, women, and children everywhere may have the opportunity of the abundant life.

8. PATRIOTIC OCCASIONS. It is so easy to fall into a cheap jingoism on such occasions, raising national barriers rather than establishing world friendships. The school of religion must hold high the standard of Christian citizenship. The message of the patriotic celebration should be, "My country, may she always be right, just, and brotherly, and may I have the courage as a citizen to help to build the ideals of Jesus into our community and national life!"

Chapter XI

TESTING THE SPIRITUAL RESULTS

What are the objectives by which the success of the Sunday School should be measured? The International Council of Religious Education has adopted a statement of objectives of religious education, falling into seven main divisions, which may be summarized as follows:

1. Consciousness of God and relationship to him.

2. An understanding and appreciation of the personality, life, and teaching of Jesus and a conscious acceptance of him and loyalty to his cause.

3. A progressive development of Christlike character.

4. The ability and disposition to share in the building of a Christian social order.

5. The ability and disposition to participate effectively in the life and work of the church.

6. A Christian interpretation of life and the universe and the development of a Christian philosophy of life.

7. A knowledge of the Bible and other religious heritages of the race.

If these objectives be the goals of religious education, we must test the success of our Sunday Schools by the extent to which they achieve these goals. The final test is life itself. When these pupils have lived a span of their normal life, we shall know whether we have succeeded in our work. But we need some test of progress to determine here and now whether we are achieving results, so that improvement may be made where we are most weak. The superintendent must take the experimental attitude toward the work of his school.

When a superintendent approaches the work of his Sunday School in the experimental attitude, with his mind set on specific objectives to be attained, he becomes at once concerned about measures of success by which he may test its effectiveness. He must know whether his pupils are moving toward the desired goal. This is difficult. To find out how fast a boy can run we need but to let him run and take his time with a stop watch. To find out how well he can read we need only let him read selections of varying degrees of difficulty. To find out how much he loves God, or his fellow man—how shall we go about that?

In a very real sense we are actually measuring character every day. We form our estimate of the boys and girls in our classes. We speak of our acquaintances as "devout," "good," "irreligious," and "Christian gentlemen." Some we would trust with our money, while some we would not trust. It is true that we are often mistaken in our estimates. But there must be some symptoms by which we evaluate character. It would seem, then, that if we could but refine our crude methods for judging character we should be on the road toward tests of moral and religious growth.

THE VALUE OF TESTING

The value of testing the work of the Sunday School is threefold:

1. IT HELPS THE PUPIL. It leads him to see that his work is considered important. It helps him to determine whether or not he has made progress. It enables him to achieve a feeling of satisfaction if his work has been well done, and a feeling of failure and of a need for improvement if he has not taken his task seriously. It helps him to distinguish the important elements in the work of the Sunday School, and to measure his competence in them.

2. IT HELPS THE TEACHER. The results of an examination are a test of the teacher as well as a test of the pupil. Failure on the part of pupils spells failure, also, for the work of teachers. Moreover, an examination shows not only the progress the pupil has made in the mastery of his work but also the points at which his needs are greatest. To test the pupil's understanding of their work will help the teacher to see his whole responsibility in the proper perspective.

3. IT HELPS THE WHOLE SCHOOL. The superintendent and the board of religious education should know what success the school is having in promoting the development of Christlike character. Tests con-

stitute a measurement of the value of the curriculum and of the competence of the teachers. Reliable tests furnish the data for a diagnosis, on the basis of which a remedy for ineffective teaching may be prescribed.

In this evaluation of the use of tests it has been assumed that we have reliable ways of estimating the success of religious teaching. Unfortunately we are still far from having a series of tests which may be generally applied by Sunday Schools.

EARMARKS OF SUCCESSFUL WORK [1]

There are certain general tests which every conscientious leader applies to his work. Many of these have some real value, if used with discrimination. Let us look at a few of the earmarks of success:

1. One of the first which occurs to us is the pupil's interest in his work, and in religious subjects generally. If he listens attentively, asks intelligent questions, and answers questions with a mark of understanding, we assume that his religious life is growing happily and that our work with him has been well done. A Church School which can develop such an interest that it will manifest itself even in the home will win the eternal praises of every parent for its efficiency and success.

[1] The substance of this section, as well as a few other paragraphs in this chapter, is taken from the much more extensive discussion of the subject in Chapter XI of the author's "Teaching for Christian Living," and is used here by permission of the publishers (Christian Board of Publication, Saint Louis, 1929).

2. One of the conspicuous ways in which interest manifests itself is in good attendance and in punctuality. Ask any teacher to rate his pupils on the basis of the effectiveness of his teaching with them, and the probability is that he will rate high those who have made the best record in attendance.

3. As another mark of success, lesson preparation will come in for large consideration. The teacher likes the pupil who may be depended on to do the work assigned and to come to class regularly with a prepared lesson.

4. Almost without exception, Sunday School teachers would rate high as a mark of successful teaching the knowledge which the pupil has acquired. Some teachers have had the courage to give their pupils searching examinations to determine the effectiveness with which the Bible has been learned. Such efforts are good, and it is to be deplored that not more of this sort of testing has been done. We must, of course, remember that there are more important tests than mere Bible knowledge. The ultimate test is character and conduct. Yet it is a good policy to assume that unless teaching leads to a definite broadening of the horizons of knowledge, it is not likely to yield much extension of the scope and quality of attitudes and habits.

5. Since the final test of the success of religious education is life, there are good reasons for looking to the daily conduct of pupils for evidence of suc-

cessful teaching. The observation of pupils in home, school, and community, under proper conditions, is one of the best tests of results achieved. To a certain extent this has always been done by teachers. Observation of life outside of the school is very difficult, though any teacher will be quick to seize upon every manifestation that his teaching is bearing fruit in conduct. Some teachers have sensed the opportunity of keeping a check on conduct effects through close association with the home.

6. Definite confession of Christ, and alignment with the Church, is to most teachers the supreme test. It is difficult for any individual teacher to apply this, because confession of Christ and joining the Church are the culmination of the work of many teachers. All teachers may take credit for the pupils who gloriously pass this test and all should share the blame with others for those pupils who fail.

These are some of the common-sense tests which we apply to measure the success of Christian teaching. The very fact that a teacher has a sufficiently critical attitude toward his work to wish to estimate its success, is in itself a wholesome sign. He must make his judgment on the basis of the best evidence he has.

The criticism to be brought against basing estimates of success on such tests as these is that the tests are usually very superficially and uncritically applied. Christian personality, manifesting itself in Christlike living, is the ultimate result for which we are striving. The results described are taken as symptoms of the existence of this ultimate value. We may so easily be mistaken in the interpretation of these symptoms. We can see only the outward signs of the inner purpose and motive and we may so easily be misled when we judge the motive by the act. Yet man must continue to form his judgments on the basis of outward symptoms, for only God is able to look directly on the inmost heart and soul and know persons as they are.

WRITTEN EXAMINATIONS

It is a surprising fact that, while public schools have probably overdone the matter of examinations, few Sunday Schools have ever attempted this method of testing their work. In recent years the value of examinations has been questioned, and there are some who advocate that they be entirely abolished. A more sane view is that examinations must be greatly reformed, but that some form of testing will probably be continued.

It seems to the author that teachers should be encouraged to give written tests to their pupils. Such tests provide an accounting on the work which teachers and pupils have done together. They help to give the pupil the impression that his work is worth while. They enable the teacher to see whether any values which the pupil is able to put on paper have resulted from his work. The results of such examinations may form the basis for reports to the home.

SCIENTIFIC TESTS

The contribution which science has made to the testing of moral and religious growth is that of refining the crude, common-sense measures which everyone is using. Scientific tests come closer to measuring the ultimate value for which we are striving, and help to avoid some of the false interpretations which we make all too easily on the basis of inaccurate and insufficient data. Scientific tests are based on the principle of "sampling" the pupil's ability in whichever direction the test is to be made. By testing a large number of pupils it becomes possible to establish standard scores or "norms," showing what pupils of a given age should be able to do. Standard tests which have been prepared for general use can be secured in printed form with accompanying directions for administration and scoring.

Space does not permit us here to discuss in detail the various types of scientific tests, or to name any specific available tests. Superintendents who plan to use this type of test must carry their study of them beyond the pages of this book.[1] Available tests may be classified as follows:

---

[1] Consult Watson, "Experimentation and Measurement in Religious Education." Information concerning available tests may be secured from "Test Service," Room 807, 347 Madison Avenue, New York City, and from the Bureau of Research, International Council of Religious Education, 203 North Wabash Avenue, Chicago, Illinois.

1. Tests of knowledge, usually Biblical knowledge, to determine the pupil's mastery of the subject matter of religious education. A knowledge of the Bible should be one of the outcomes of religious education, and such knowledge is therefore a legitimate field for testing. Undoubtedly the knowledge of the Bible could be greatly improved through a proper use of such tests. Our more recent emphasis on character as over against Biblical knowledge has to some extent retarded the development of tests in this field. Used with proper caution, however, Biblical knowledge tests are a great aid to the work of the Church School.

2. Tests of moral knowledge and judgment, to determine to what extent a pupil is able to think his way through moral situations. Right knowledge is an important element in right conduct. Tests of moral knowledge and ethical judgment are important because they reveal the pupil's ability in this field. If knowledge is faulty or incorrect the teacher has a chance to center his teaching where it is most needed. Caution should be exercised here, however, that we do not assume that when a pupil knows what is right he will always act according to his best knowledge.

3. Tests of religious ideas, to determine what a pupil thinks about God and religious subjects. It goes without saying that a person's understanding of the character and purpose of God, and his

general idea of what it means to be religious, will to some extent determine his conduct in life situations. If we know the religious ideas held by our pupils it is possible to encourage those which are right and to correct those which are wrong.

4. Tests of attitudes, to determine how a pupil feels about certain situations. Attitudes are important determiners of conduct. If we know how a person feels about a given question, we may pretty accurately predict how he will act. A very important step in good teaching is to find out what the attitudes of one's pupils are. It is difficult to measure attitudes because it is hard to express them in terms of quantity. It is important, however, that progress be made in this field.

5. Tests of conduct, to determine what a person will actually do when he faces problems of right and wrong. This is perhaps the most effective measure of the pupil's competence in Christian living, but tests of this kind are very hard to devise and give. It is difficult to plan situations in which the pupil may be tested without his knowing that he is being tested. It is difficult also to test him in a sufficient number of situations to be sure of what may be expected of him in all situations. Nevertheless, it is well to keep centering our thought on what the pupil actually does as we attempt to measure the effectiveness of our teaching.

THE SUPERINTENDENT'S ADMINISTRATION OF TESTS

What should be the superintendent's attitude toward the testing of results in the Sunday School? If he sets himself definitely to bring about improvement in teaching he cannot avoid giving some attention to the results of teaching.

One thing which every superintendent can do is to develop the experimental attitude on the part of himself and his workers. By this is meant the attitude of looking for results and of utilizing methods so that the best results may be achieved. Too many workers are going on year after year assuming that they are doing satisfactory work without ever taking the trouble to examine themselves and their work critically in order to decide whether all is being accomplished that might be. A school which has developed the experimental attitude toward its own work is likely to be a school which will improve its work.

A second thing which every superintendent may do is to encourage workers to measure the results of their own work. This will involve looking for results in the lives of pupils in such ways as we have discussed under the heading "common-sense measures," and giving such simple examinations as may be feasible. Most workers will need some help in preparing and scoring such examinations. Care should be taken that the right attitude is developed on the part of the pupils before examinations are attempted.

A third thing which some superintendents will be ready to do is to look into the possibility of using standard tests in the Sunday School. This is a step which should be taken with caution. The untrained person has no more right to attempt to diagnose the spiritual well-being of pupils by means of these delicate instruments than the untrained person has to assume the rôle of a physician and attempt to diagnose the physical well-being of persons. Any Sunday School which is ready to venture into this field of standard tests should first secure some one who will make a careful study of the meaning and use of them, and, if possible, take a course in the administration of tests. It may sometimes be possible to enlist the services of a teacher from the public-school system who is skilled in the use of tests. The author's advice would be to move into this field as soon as possible, but to move with great caution and only after making sure that there are competent workers under whose direction the tests will be administered.

Chapter XII

THE EXPANDING PROGRAM

Usually the chief executive officer in the Sunday School is a superintendent who must share with the pastor and other competent workers the task of supervision. We have discussed the problem of supervision from the standpoint of the Sunday School, not because we maintain that the traditional Sunday School with its one-hour sessions constitutes an adequate program of religious education but because we desire this book to be of greatest helpfulness to the large majority of churches. The greatest need of these churches is the improvement of their Sunday Schools. An efficient Sunday School is the best foundation on which to build a more extensive program of work. Let us in this final chapter take a look at the expanding program and what it involves from the standpoint of supervision.

It requires no argument to convince most people that religious education cannot be adequately carried on with but one hour a week of time. We must recognize that life is very complex and that adequate guidance for Christian living can hardly be given by means of a few admonitions in a single hour a week. One of the ideals of the superintendent should be, therefore, the expansion of the work of his school beyond this traditional one-hour period.

It is inevitable that religious education in a progressive church will extend beyond the boundaries of the Sunday School period. Many types of activities will grow out of the life of the Sunday School. This lays upon the superintendent an obligation to assure proper supervision for such activities as may not actually take place during the Sunday period when he is officially on duty.

DEVELOPING AN EDUCATIONALLY MINDED CHURCH

The first consideration in moving toward a larger program of religious education is to make the program an expression of the work of the entire church. The school must be not simply in the church but also of the church. The supervisor should, therefore, give much attention to the problem of "selling" religious education to the church.

A few years ago when the primary business of the nation was war, everyone seemed to be imbued with the spirit of doing his part for his nation. The idea was in the atmosphere and a man could no more escape it than he could escape being in some communication with his fellow beings. Just so, when the primary business of a church is recognized to be that of education, the educational ideal will take hold of the members of that church.

Let us consider a few suggestions concerning ways

in which the superintendent may help to develop an educationally minded church:

1. BY MAGNIFYING THE EDUCATIONAL PROGRAM. There should be a place for everyone in the school of religion, and everyone should have repeated invitations to take advantage of that which has been provided for him. Let us get over the notion that the Church School is for children only. Let us implant the ideal that spiritual growth through religious education is a thing to be desired by every Christian.

2. BY KEEPING THE SCHOOL BEFORE THE WHOLE CHURCH THROUGH SPECIAL SERVICES AND REGULAR REPORTS. There are occasions when the work of religious education should form the normal content of church activities. The installation and commissioning service for the workers, Graduation and Promotion Sunday, Christmas and Easter activities, Children's Day—all are occasions on which the work of the Church School may normally be brought into the church service. And let it be emphasized that the purpose of such services is not to "show off" the children or to amuse the adults. They are occasions when the church's attention is normally centered on religious education.

Reports on the work of the school should be brought as a matter of course to the business meetings of the congregation. This is simply a way in which the officers may give an account of the work which has been intrusted to them. In addition, items of particular importance in the work of religious education should be brought before the congregation through the pulpit, the bulletin board, items in the newspaper, and the use of the church calendar or parish paper.

3. By Recognizing the Church's Financial Responsibility for Its School of Religious Education. When religious education is thought of as one of the major responsibilities of the church, it is right that it should appear in the church budget. It is not right that pupils should be asked to finance the school. Many of them make contributions to the general church budget. To be sure, we should avoid pauperizing the members of the school by giving them everything free of charge. Each member should be given an opportunity to contribute to the work of the church as a whole, thus emphasizing the fact that membership in any branch of the church's work should give a sense of belonging to the church as a whole.

4. By Enlisting the Pastor's Interest and Support. As the pastor is so will the church be. While there are many churches in which progressive work in religious education has been developed without the aid of an interested pastor, these are the exception rather than the rule. The pastor is the head of the church, and the church must look to him for guidance in the development of its entire program of work. There are many ways in which the

pastor may aid the cause of religious education. He can help best of all if he himself assumes responsibility for the educational direction of the school. Increasingly pastors are assuming such responsibility and acting as their own directors of religious education. Even when this is not necessary, the pastor's active interest in the cause of religious education, his representation of it before the congregation, his support of those who are carrying active responsibilities, his attention to matters of religious education as he goes about his pastoral visits, will enable him to accomplish what no other person in the church can accomplish. The superintendent's first concern should be to work in close harmony and coöperation with his pastor.

5. By Putting the School Under the Direction of a Board of Religious Education. This plan was fully discussed in Chapter II.

TYPES OF OUTREACH

When we speak of expanding the program of religious education we cannot think simply of one type of organization. There is no best way to approach this problem. Some churches are ready for one type of program and some for another. It is to the credit of religious education that in the expansion of its work beyond the Sunday School it has shown great vitality in building on needs and conditions as they exist locally. Here are a few of

the ways in which the program of religious education
has been broadened:

1. OUTSIDE ACTIVITIES OF CLASSES AND GROUPS.
It is inevitable that groups of boys and girls meeting as Sunday School classes and departments should
desire to participate in activities through the week.
These activities may be of various sorts. Sometimes
they lead to the organization of athletic teams or to
departmental or class socials or picnics and outings
for departments, classes, or the whole school. Many
churches have service groups of various types, such
as missionary organizations; in other churches the
older boys and girls have been organized into groups
such as Boy Scouts and Camp Fire Girls. Occasionally churches have dramatic groups, and in most
schools there is enough interest in dramatic activities
to make possible the presentation of a play or
pageant on special occasions.

Sometimes these outside activities are the spon-
taneous outgrowth of the Sunday School and
sometimes they are set in motion by outside agencies
without relation to the Sunday School. It is desirable
that the interests of the Sunday School be broadened
to include activities beyond those which can be carried out on Sunday. It is very important, however,
that the activities be definitely related to the Sunday
School and that they be under competent supervision. An athletic team without a competent supervisor may be more of a liability than an asset.

Wherever possible the teacher or leader in the Sunday School should share with his pupils in these outside activities.

2. Young People's Societies. In most churches there is an organization of young people, meeting on Sunday evening. The work of such Young People's Societies is a distinct contribution to religious education. While such societies are usually independent of the Sunday School, there should be a close inter-relationship. When religious education is organized on the larger basis, under a church board of religious education, such societies as well as the Sunday School should be under the general supervision of this board.

3. The Expanded Session. This term has been given to the effort which is being made in a considerable number of churches to increase the time available for religious education by extending the Sunday School through the Sunday-morning period from 9.30 or 10 until noon. When this is done, emphasis is laid on the fact that there is no contrast between "Sunday School" and "church." Whatever is done is done by the entire church in action. If the Juniors meet throughout the Sunday-morning period, they are not being deprived of going to "church" but are simply the Junior Department of the church in action.

It is readily apparent that this plan provides a long enough period of time to make possible a constructive program which includes various types of activities. To make such a plan effective requires very competent leadership. It requires more attention to supervision than is ordinarily given. However, when churches are able to launch an expanded type of program, they should not hesitate to take this significant step.

4. THE VACATION CHURCH SCHOOL. Churches are more and more using the summer vacation period for religious education. Vacation Church Schools usually continue through a period of from three to five weeks and meet five mornings in the week for from two and a half to three hours. Such schools are planned to provide various types of activities, and experience proves that the schools are sufficiently interesting to children to draw them even in vacation time. Hence the Vacation Church School offers an opportunity for doubling the time which may be devoted to religious education in any year.

It will usually not be possible for the superintendent of the Sunday School to serve also as leader of the Vacation Church School, or for most of the teachers to work in the Vacation School. The two types of schools should, however, be very closely related, and the work done in one school should take account of the work done in the other. Adequate supervision for the Church School will provide for this type of relationship. An employed director of religious education and a board of religious education in the local church are suggested as the best method of relating these two phases of work in an effective way.

5. THE WEEK DAY CHURCH SCHOOL. This is an expansion of religious education into week days. Usually the Week Day Church School meets on "released time," that is, on time provided by an arrangement with the public school whereby pupils are dismissed for certain hours in the week for religious education. Often the Week Day Church School is conducted interdenominationally, in order to provide greater strength in securing pupils, equipping buildings, and employing competent teachers.

It is desirable that the Sunday School and the Week Day Church School be closely related. If the teachers of the Sunday School can be secured to give an additional period during the week and thus carry on continuous work with their classes, the problem will be solved. One church met its problem in this way: About half the Sunday School pupils attended the Week Day School. On Sunday each grade was divided into two groups so as to put all those who attended Week Day School into one class and all those who attended only the Sunday School into another class, boys and girls mixed. The teachers who were able to teach a week-day period in addition to the Sunday period were placed in charge of the former, while other teachers were placed in charge of the latter.

Where it is impossible to carry over the teaching

personnel of the Sunday School into the Week Day School, other provisions must be made for keeping a very close contact between the work of the two. The board of religious education can do much in bringing this about.

6. THE HOME. It is, of course, not entirely correct to say that the Sunday School may expand its scope to include the home. The home itself is the most important school of religious education. What we have in mind is that the effectiveness of the work which the Sunday School is doing may be greatly increased through proper coöperation with the home. If parents but knew what the Sunday School is attempting to accomplish with their children, they would be in a position to assist in producing the desired results.

Proper coöperation between the Sunday School and the home requires that the teachers shall visit the homes of the pupils, that report cards on the work which pupils are doing shall be sent to the homes, that parents shall be invited to the Sunday School to observe the work which is being done and to parent-teacher meetings to discuss the problems of religious education. It should require further that the pastor in his pastoral visits stress the importance of Christian nurture in the home and help to interpret the work of the Church School to parents.

7. THE CHURCH SCHOOL. When religious education in the local church has been expanded in some

of the ways suggested above, we can no longer speak of the educational organization as the Sunday School. It has passed beyond the stage of work done on Sunday. It has become the church engaged in the work of education. We now speak of it as the Church School. The Sunday School now is an element in a total program, and may be called the Sunday Church School to distinguish it from the Week Day Church School, and the Vacation Church School.

SUPERVISING THE EXPANDING PROGRAM

The work of supervision in religious education must expand as the Church School expands. Certain phases of this supervisory program may here be emphasized:

1. Constant effort must be exerted to make and keep the Church School the expression of the interest and work of the church. We have discussed this problem in the section dealing with the development of an educationally minded church.

2. The program of religious education must be properly integrated so as to assure the greatest religious growth on the part of the pupil. In many churches various types of independent organizations have sprung up so that pupils are torn between loyalties. They are hurried from one meeting to another, with insufficient time for effective work. Sometimes these various organizations duplicate each other's work, while certain important elements in religious

education are neglected. Proper supervision of the expanding program of religious education will enable each phase to render its contribution to a larger whole. Thus each part of the program makes its own contribution to the total education of the child.

3. Those who supervise must give attention to making and keeping the various activities of the Church School worth while and proper. There are so many things which may be done with the precious minutes during which the church has the child. Often the more serious work is turned aside to make room for all kinds of fads and frills which have been introduced in the name of religious education. Many activities are carried on which cannot possibly contribute to religious growth. At times activities have been launched which have been positively harmful to the child's religious development. All the while great, valuable things which ought to be done may have been neglected. Supervisors must view the whole program and enable each phase of it to make its maximum contribution.

4. The superintendent, as the leader in developing the church's larger educational work, must have in mind constantly that each new phase as it is added should be placed under competent leadership and related to the whole undertaking. We must recognize frankly that the layman superintendent cannot supervise the total educational program which should be fostered by a modern church. This means that

he must be a man who is large enough in spirit to relinquish leadership here and there to other persons. Yet he will not build soundly unless he erects a larger structure in which each phase of the school, including the Sunday session, may find its life. We have suggested that the board of religious education of the local church is the means toward responsible supervision for such a program.

THE TEST OF SUPERVISION

Throughout these chapters we have maintained that the purpose of the Sunday School must be growth in Christian living. Improvement in teaching is desired in order that growth may take place more rapidly and more effectively. Good administration and effective supervision will build an impressive organization and develop a worthy program. Let us keep constantly in mind, however, that the final test is not more activities, more teachers, larger buildings, more pupils, or better equipment. The test of supervision is the effectiveness of the school in promoting growth in Christian living.

APPENDIX A

A SERVICE OF PERSONAL DEDICATION [1]

For the Commissioning of Teachers and Officers

This service of personal dedication is planned for use in a regular public service of worship, but as the order of such services varies greatly in the several Communions no attempt is made here to develop a complete order for the whole service. These suggestions may readily be incorporated in the regular order of the church. This service might well be printed in the regular church calendar where there is one, or mimeographed, or copied in some other way.

At the proper point in the regular service of worship the following features may be introduced:

MINISTER: It is a part of the plan of God that the richest lessons and the deepest things of life are passed on from those who are more mature to those who are less mature. So we have the work of teachers in the world.

For this reason, our church has recently chosen those who are to be the teachers and leaders in our Church School for the coming year. We have come together at this time to set aside these people to the sacred task which they are to undertake in our name.

Those who have been elected as officers will please stand.

(*The officers elect rise.*)

---

[1] Prepared by P. R. Hayward for the International Journal of Religious Education, and reproduced here by permission of the author and the publishers.

MINISTER: To the holy ministry of business details and to the sanctified service of unseen drudgery,

OFFICERS: We dedicate ourselves, O Lord.

MINISTER: To the spiritual values that lie in a wise routine,

OFFICERS: We dedicate ourselves, O Lord.

MINISTER: To farsighted plans and wise counsels for bringing in thy Kingdom,

OFFICERS: We dedicate ourselves, O Lord.

MINISTER: Do you pledge to the fulfillment of these sacred obligations the utmost of your hand and brain and inner self, in the spirit and presence of Christ?

OFFICERS: We do.

MINISTER: Those who have been elected as teachers will please stand.

(The teachers elect rise, while the officers remain standing.)

MINISTER: For the children and youth of our church and for their eager responsiveness to all that is good and beautiful and true,

TEACHERS: We give, Lord, our hearty thanks.

MINISTER: For insight to sense their inward selves, for patience to wait the full fruitage of truth in their lives, for wisdom in understanding the paths that thy feet follow in the complete redemption of a growing life,

TEACHERS: We earnestly beseech thee, O Lord.

MINISTER: To the fulfillment in these lines of divine command, "Go . . . teaching,"

TEACHERS: We dedicate ourselves, O Lord.

Appendix A

Minister: Do you pledge to the fulfillment of these sacred obligations the utmost of your hand and brain and inner self, in the spirit and presence of Christ?

Teachers: We do.

Minister: The members of the congregation will please stand.

(*All rise, while the officers and teachers remain standing.*)

Minister: As the parents and friends of our boys and girls to whose service these teachers and leaders have now been set aside,

Congregation: We now pledge to them our loyal support, our sympathetic coöperation in the home, our patience and good will in their holy work.

Minister: In accord with the regulations of this church and by the authority vested in me as a minister of Jesus Christ, I hereby solemnly commission you as teachers and officers to serve in the high privilege of Christian education in the ———————— Church School.

Prayer:

"O teach me, Lord, that I may teach
The precious things thou dost impart;
And wing my words, that they may reach
The hidden depths of many a heart."

Response by Choir:

Lord, pour out thy spirit from on high
And these thy willing servants bless;
Graces and gifts to each supply
And clothe them with thy righteousness.

APPENDIX B

A CONSTITUTION FOR THE CHURCH SCHOOL

This constitution is presented here as an example rather than as a model. It grew out of the needs of a church which is facing the development of a comprehensive program of religious education, though at present it has little more than the usual Sunday School. The constitution has served the needs of this church well.

Every church should frame its constitution to meet its own needs. Let this therefore serve more as a thought starter than as a guide.

CONSTITUTION

ARTICLE I. NAME

The name of this organization shall be The Church School of the Evangelical Saint Peter's Church in Elmhurst, Illinois.

ARTICLE II. PURPOSE

The Church School shall carry on all the work of Saint Peter's Church which is of a strictly educational nature. Specifically, this will include the Sunday School, catechetical instruction classes, the Vacation Church School, the Week Day Church School, Young People's clubs and societies, the Home Department and Cradle Roll, missionary organizations, and any other educational activities which may be organized.

Appendix B

Article III. Organization

Section 1—The Board of Religious Education:

(1) Responsibility for the organization and management of the Church School shall be vested in a board of religious education, elected by the church and responsible to the church. The personnel and manner of election of this board shall be as provided in the church constitution.

(2) Associate (nonvoting) members may be designated by the board of religious education.

(3) The board of religious education shall meet at least monthly, for not less than ten months in the year.

Section 2—Officers of the Church School:

(1) The *pastor* of the church is the ranking officer of the Church School.

(2) The *director of religious education* is a salaried officer who has responsibility for the administration of the program of religious education, under the direction of the board of religious education. He is the executive officer of this board. In case no director of religious education is employed by the church, the chairman of the board of religious education shall act in this capacity.

(3) The *secretary of records and supplies* shall (*a*) keep a progressive record of the work and progress of each pupil in the school, and supervise the keeping of proper records in each department and class; keep a file of prospective members; record such items concerning the educational program as will be to the best interest of the school, and keep the various officers informed concerning progress and needs in their respective depart-

ments of work; (*b*) purchase, file, and dispense as needed, the literature and other supplies of the school, on order of the board of religious education or an authorized officer of the school.

(4) The *treasurer* shall be the custodian of all funds of the school, have general charge of offerings and give out such information as will promote the best education in Christian giving, and pay the financial obligations of the school when these are presented as properly approved bills. When the budget shall have become a part of the general church budget, the treasurer shall work in collaboration with the treasurer of the church.

(5) *Other officers* may be chosen as needed.

Article IV. Finances

Section 1—Budget:

A budget for the Church School shall be prepared and adopted annually by the board of religious education. Proper provision shall be made in this budget for all phases of the educational program.

Section 2—Expenditures:

All major new expenditures shall be approved by the board of religious education before they are incurred. Routine and incidental expenditures shall be left to the discretion of the officers for each phase of the program. Bills shall be paid by the treasurer when they have been approved by the superintendent of the phase of the program (e. g., Sunday School, Young People's Society, etc.) for which incurred, and the director of religious education or chairman of the board of religious education.

Appendix B

ARTICLE V. THE SPECIFIC PHASES OF THE CHURCH SCHOOL

Section 1—The Sunday School:

(1) The *superintendent* shall be the chief executive and administrative officer of the Sunday School, and responsible to the board of religious education for carrying out its program. He shall be elected annually by the board of religious education.

(2) *Principals of departments* shall be elected annually by the board of religious education, on nomination of the superintendent, for each of the departments of the Sunday School meeting as a separate unit. Each shall be responsible for the administration and supervision of a unified program of religious education in his department.

(3) *Class teachers* and other *officers of departments,* as needed, shall be elected annually by the board of religious education on nomination of the principal of each department through the superintendent.

Section 2—the Vacation Church School:

(1) The *principal* shall be the chief executive and administrative officer of the Vacation Church School, and responsible to the board of religious education for the carrying out of its program. He shall be elected annually by the board of religious education.

(2) *Leaders of departments* and *teachers* for the Vacation Church School shall be elected annually by the board of religious education, on nomination of the principal.

Section 3—The Week Day Church School:

(1) The *principal* shall be the chief executive and administrative officer of the Week Day Church School, and responsible to the board of religious education for the carrying out of its program. He shall be elected annually by the board of religious education.

(2) *Leaders of departments* and *teachers* for the Week Day Church School shall be elected annually by the board of religious education, on nomination of the principal.

(3) In case there is an interdenominational Week Day Church School, coöperation shall be sought as provided in Article VI.

Section 4—Catechetical Instruction:

Catechetical instruction shall be in the charge of the *pastor,* who shall, under the direction of the board of religious education, correlate this phase of the educational program as closely as possible with the entire work of the Church School.

Section 5—Cradle Roll:

(1) The Cradle Roll Department shall be in the charge of a *superintendent,* elected annually by the board of religious education, and responsible to this board for the carrying out of its program.

(2) Helpers for the Cradle Roll shall be elected annually by the board of religious education, as needed, on nomination of the superintendent.

Appendix B

Section 6—Home Department:

(1) The Home Department shall be in the charge of a *superintendent,* elected annually by the board of religious education, and responsible to this board for the carrying out of its program.

(2) Helpers for the Home Department, as needed, shall be elected annually by the board of religious education, on nomination of the superintendent.

Section 7—Other Phases:

As other phases of the program of religious education develop, and it seems advisable to incorporate them into the Church School, provision shall be made for them in this constitution, in harmony with the rest of the document.

Article VI. Interchurch Activities

*Section 1—*It shall be the policy of this Church School to coöperate in worthy interchurch and community enterprises for the advancement of religious education.

*Section 2—*The Board of Religious Education shall represent Saint Peter's Church in such coöperative educational enterprises.

Article VII. Amendments

This constitution may be amended by a two-thirds vote of the members of the board of religious education.

INDEX